ON THE WAY HOME

On the Way Home is a series of public dialogues intended to forge links between psychoanalysis and other disciplines, including the physical and the social sciences, history and literature. They are held at the Institute of Psychoanalysis and attract a wide audience.

ON THE WAY HOME

Conversations between writers and
psychoanalysts

edited by
Marie Bridge

KARNAC

First published in 2008 by
Karnac Books Ltd.
118 Finchley Road
London NW3 5HT

British Library Cataloguing in Publication Data
A C.I.P. for this book is available from the British Library

ISBN-13: 978-1-85575-683-0

Edited, designed, and produced by Florence Production Ltd,
www.florenceproduction.co.uk

Printed and bound in Great Britain by Biddles Ltd.

www.karnacbooks.com

CONTENTS

The third carriage contained Arthur Mold, Albert Ward, Charles Smith and George Yates.

The fourth carriage Mr F. Sugg, Mr R J. Southworth and Mr J. Starr (Widnes).

The fifth carriage Mr Joseph Parkenance, Mr Rogers, Mr George Waters and the Rev. McNought.

The sixth and last carriage contained Alderman Quinn, Counsellors T. Laws, W. Palin and T. Smith representing Widnes Corporation.

The funeral procession moved off slowly dispersing the large crowd somewhat, it moved into Henrietta Street where there was almost as many people waiting to see the cortège pass.

The footpaths and roadsides were filled with people. Many local residents had drawn their curtains and all the men raised their hats out of respect as the cortège passed. There were many floral wreaths, with those from the Lancashire Cricket Club and Stoddart on the side of the hearse, reminding the people who attended the funeral that "a great master of cricket was going to his last resting place".

There were many wreaths from all over the Country, amongst the most beautiful floral tokens, was one sent by Mr and Mrs George Yates. Three cricket stumps of hyacinths were held together at the top by bails of violets and across the wicket there was a bat composed of the same flowers. There was a harp of exceptional size from the Broughton Rangers Football Club and a wreath composed of bay-leaves only, tied with long red and white streamers from Mr George Robey, the comedian and personal friend of Johnny.

A huge crowd assembled at the cemetery about 30 minutes before the internment; by the time the people who had travelled by special train and buses had arrived, the crowd was estimated to be at least 2,000, the cortège arrived at the cemetery

ACKNOWLEDGEMENTS

I would like to thank Brenda Maddox, Philip Pullman, Rose Tremain, A.S. Byatt and the *British Journal of Psychotherapy* for permission to quote from:

Brenda Maddox, *D.H. Lawrence, The Story of a Marriage*, New York, Simon and Schuster, 1994

Brenda Maddox, *George's Ghosts: A New Life of W.B. Yeats*, New York, Picador, 1999

Philip Pullman, *His Dark Materials*, New York, Random House, 2006

Rose Tremain, *Sacred Country*, published by Sinclair-Stevenson/ Vintage, London, 1992 © The Random House Group. Reprinted by permission of The Random House Group Ltd.

A.S. Byatt, The Biographer's Tale, published by Chatto & Windus. Vintage, London, 2000 © The Random House Group. Reprinted by permission of The Random House Group Ltd.

Schimmel, P. (2000). "It is myself that I remake": W.B. Yeats's Self Construction in Life and Poetry. *British Journal of Psychotherapy*, 17(1): 71–84.

On the Way Home was devised and organised by a group of analysts at the Institute of Psychoanalysis without whose vision and enthusiasm these dialogues would not have taken place. My thanks are due to this group and especially to the series co-ordinator, Ruth Robinson, whose insistence and determination made things happen that might otherwise have remained just good ideas. I also wish to thank the staff at the Institute, especially Ann Glynn and Nick Hall, for making everything run so smoothly. Many people were involved in editing the dialogues: Claire Clayton made the original transcription; John Churcher, David Mayers and Ken Robinson helped with copy-editing. Sara Flanders and Caroline Garland read and approved the text for publication. I cannot thank sufficiently the authors and discussants: it is one thing for a busy author or analyst to agree to do the dialogue but quite another to give precious time to the work of editing. Finally, I thank all four generations of my family for their tolerance of my "impossible profession" and, above all, my husband for his ever generous encouragement.

Marie Bridge

CONTRIBUTORS

NICOLA ABEL-HIRSCH is a Member of the Institute of Psycho-analysis. She is the author of *Eros* (Icon Books, 2001) and a number of papers on the work of Wilfred Bion. She works in private practice in London.

MARIE BRIDGE studied modern languages at Oxford. She is a Training Analyst at the Institute of Psychoanalysis and an Honorary Senior Lecturer at the University of Essex. She is in full time private practice in East Anglia.

A.S. BYATT is the author of several novels, books of short stories and criticism. Her works are translated into at least 28 languages. Her most recent novel is *A Whistling Woman (2002)* and this was followed by *The Little Black Book of Stories (2003)*. (Both published by Chatto and Windus.)

JOHN CHURCHER is a psychoanalyst in Manchester, and a Member of the Institute of Psychoanalysis. He studied philosophy and psychology at Oxford, and was for many years a Lecturer in Psychology at the University of Manchester.

BRENDA MADDOX is a prize-winning biographer of, among others, Nora Joyce, D. H. Lawrence and Rosalind Franklin ("The Dark Lady of DNA"). Her latest book is *Freud's Wizard: the Enigma of Ernest Jones*, published by John Murray Ltd (2006) and by Da Capo Press (2007).

PHILIP PULLMAN is the author of several novels and fairy tales. His best known work is the trilogy *His Dark Materials*, which has been translated into 38 languages and was recently adapted for the stage by the National Theatre. The final part of the trilogy, *The Amber Spyglass*, was the only children's novel ever to win the Whitbread Book of the Year award.

RUTH ROBINSON is a Member of the Institute of Psychoanalysis and a psychoanalyst working in private practice in London.

IGNÊS SODRÉ trained as a clinical psychologist in Rio de Janeiro and came to London in 1969 to do the psychoanalytic training at the British Psychoanalytical Society. She is a Training Analyst. She has taught extensively here and abroad, and has published many papers on psychoanalysis and on literature. She co-authored a book with A.S. Byatt, *Imagining Characters*.

JENNY STOKER is a psychoanalyst who works with adults and children in private practice as well as at the Anna Freud Centre. She is a Fellow of the Institute of Psychoanalysis. She also teaches and writes. She is the author of a book for parents about toddler development, *You and Your Toddler*.

HELEN TAYLOR ROBINSON is a Fellow of the Institute of Psychoanalysis and a child and adult analyst in full time private practice. She has lectured and published on art and psychoanalysis, teaching at UCL and BPC organisations. Her most recent publication is an article in *Sex and Sexuality: Winnicottian Perspectives*, edited by L. Caldwell (Karnac, 2005).

ROSE TREMAIN's *Restoration* was shortlisted for the Booker Prize. *Sacred Country* won the Prix Femina Etranger, and *Music and Silence* the Whitbread Novel of the Year Award. Her novels have been published in 22 countries. *Restoration* was filmed in 1995 and films of *Music and Silence* and *The Colour* are now in development. Her most recent publication was an acclaimed new collection from Chatto and Windus, *The Darkness of Wallis Simpson*.

MARGOT WADDELL is a fellow of the Institue of Psychoanalysis and a Consultant Child and Adolescent Psychotherapist in the Adolescent Department of the Tavistock Clinic, London. She is the author of many articles, both clinical and literary, and her most recent book, *Inside Lives: Psychoanalysis and the Development of the Personality*, was published by Karnac in 2002.

Introduction

Marie Bridge

Literature was present at the birth of psychoanalysis. When Freud made his momentous discovery of the Oedipus complex within himself and his patients, he recognised that this psychic configuration had already been depicted in Sophocles's tragedy. He attributed the "gripping power of *Oedipus Rex*" to the unconscious recognition of our own incestuous desires and murderous wishes towards our parents. But Freud only discovered the unconscious in the sense that Columbus discovered America: like America, it was always there. The father of psychoanalysis wrote: "The poets and philosophers before me discovered the unconscious . . . What I discovered was [only] the scientific method by which the unconscious might be studied."

These dialogues bring together authors whose work similarly provokes recognition and resonance in the minds of readers; analysts with a professional and passionate interest in the unconscious and a wish to learn from writers; and a wide audience of people interested in literature and psychoanalysis. The authors who agreed to share these dialogues were invited by analysts with a particular interest in their work. Some were already interested in psychoanalytic ideas; others had almost no familiarity with the subject and even some scepticism. The analysts are not interested in psychologising about the authors; if anything, they are rather shy of discussing the authors' personal lives, even when the authors speak of it themselves. The interest is in a non-specialist exploration of the writing, in the process of writing, in engaging with literature as a reader, and in areas of commonality and difference between psychoanalysis and literature.

Each dialogue has its own unique character. Alongside the main interlocutors, other individual voices can be clearly distinguished in the developing conversations. For the Pullman dialogue there were many children and young people in the audience, including a girl who so doggedly refused, day after day, to accept "sold out" for an answer that she was rewarded with a free ticket. In each conversation the personal chemistry between the discussants gives the dialogue its charge, whether the participants are old friends like Byatt and Sodré or have only met once before to explore possible areas of discussion. Moments of tension, disagreement, misunderstanding, or sudden illumination give the conversations their liveliness.

The authors are three novelists and a biographer. One of the biographer's subjects is a novelist (Lawrence) and one of the novelists, Byatt, is talking about her novel *The Biographer's Tale*— the biography of a biographer. Taylor Robinson points out that psychoanalysis developed out of Freud's autobiography in *The Interpretation of Dreams*. Maddox comments that biographers "have in common with psychoanalysts . . . [the need] . . . to construct a narrative." The need to tell stories and to hear stories and through stories to find meaning is universal. Indeed it is often when someone finds that "the centre cannot hold" in their own internal autobiography that they seek analysis, hoping for a more complex, more coherent and eventually truer story.

Perhaps writers who are interested in a dialogue with analysts are to some extent self-selecting. It is not only Tremain who is "much concerned with what states of mind [her] characters are in". All the participants share what Sodré describes as "a very deep desire to know more about minds". Although one of Byatt's themes is the opacity of her characters, nevertheless she comments that "no matter how clever or postmodern the novelist is, the moment the story starts moving as a tale, you start responding to the characters as people." It is not only their respect for developmental history ("the child is father of the man") that links the analyst, the biographer and these novelists. It is also that, in Tremain's words, "the emotion is the action", and it is through the stories that we learn more about minds. Pullman describes how the extraordinarily evocative idea of the daemon came to him as a device to further the narrative "in a simple, technical storytelling way". Nevertheless, even in such compelling, page-turning, exciting action adventures, the drama still turns on the internal conflicts and emotional development of the characters— the painful soul-searching conversations between Lyra and her daemon remind us of Shakespeare's soliloquies. It is above all the internal story that grips us: the discovery of "the self inside the self that we are" (Tremain); the wrestling with external-ised internal voices as Bridge discusses with Pullman; the representation of different aspects of the self that Waddell explores with Tremain.

One attraction these writers have for psychoanalysts is their emphasis on truthfulness as an attitude of mind. In *The Amber Spyglass* it is the telling of a true story that is Lyra's salvation when she faces the falsifying selective truths of the Harpies. "You have to notice the world and come down there with a story to tell; it doesn't have to be a dramatic story but it has to be true. It doesn't have to be well constructed but it has to be full of things that can feed this hunger for reality, for truth," says Pullman. Yet, as Bridge suggests to him, one thread of his trilogy is the problem of how to discern what is true from what is apparently true but perverted to serve other ends. All these authors have a capacity to convey the complexity of "true stories". "I think the truth is a very complicated thing and only the constructed object of a novel can give you an inkling of how," says Byatt.

The complex relation between truth and fiction is indeed the conscious subject of Byatt's novel *The Biographer's Tale,* as Sodré brings out clearly. "Facts slide into fictions." Byatt sees the "shifti-ness" in this novel as "something to do with liking labyrinths and mirrors, which are an image for some part of our own nature, which we can't know," or even about the "unknowability of human beings". This need for a constant revision of pers-pective is also central to psychoanalysis, as it is to life. Just as the omniscient single-voiced narrator in fiction is now distrusted, the patient too tells the analyst countless variations of the same story so that eventually the analytic couple can begin to discern which internal voices are colouring which version of the story, and the relative truthfulness of each voice. The opening chapters of Pullman's *Northern Lights* tease the reader and awaken his anxious curiosity by constantly shifting the location of "goodness". As soon as the reader feels that he has identified the "goodies" and "baddies" in the retiring room, the ground shifts and the story becomes more complicated. Sodré links this disorientation as the writer descends into the maelstrom to the necessary fragmentation that precedes putting together a new mosaic of understanding, but it also offers a potent metaphor for the experience of reading, as indeed for the enterprise of psychoanalysis, in either role. Although Byatt jibs at the notion of having "something to say" and Pullman at the idea that he is "getting at" anything, there is a moral vision, or an attitude of mind, that links these writers in their respect for truthfulness and their exploration of the difficulty in holding that position. Byatt describes the difficulty she experiences in recovering if she finds she has written something untrue. Indeed there is always the "continual wish to tell another story . . . to keep us from the real pain and hurt of life", as Taylor Robinson puts it. And of course this goes for the analyst too. One audience participant draws attention to "a link between the endeavour of the biographer and the endeavour of the analyst, in the sense that it is always trying to discover something about the other's desire, but it's always being influenced by one's own desire."

Waddell takes Tremain's central metaphor from *Music and Silence*, the musicians working in the cellar in the dark, to be a representation of both the creative process and the analytic process. The writers all convey something of the meticulous conscious crafting of their work. The analysts are also interested in the unconscious at work, the work that happens in the dark. The writers are clearly interested in this too, though they might call it by another name. Although Tremain distances herself from a "sentimental" idea of the "characters taking over", she describes how she is forced to write a different, "more truthful" ending for Merivel in *Restoration*. "If the characters are functioning as living, breathing beings for the reader, they will have an integrity that the author has to recognise and honour." Pullman lucidly conveys the technical craftsmanship of storytelling, but also goes on to describe the mysterious genesis of a brilliant idea. "Then I realised that it was only children's daemons that changed shape; adults' daemons settle down in one fixed form and stick to that. *That* was the moment when I really realised I'd got something. I remember I was walking up and down the garden thinking this through, and I remember the very stone I was standing on when this idea struck! It was the best idea I'd ever had in my life." The image of Pullman suddenly perceiving an idea as though it was in some sense "always there" chimes with Wilfred Bion's concept of "a thought waiting for a thinker". Tremain describes a similar sudden illumination on hearing about the musicians at Rosenborg: "I thought it a very beautiful image but it also seemed to me to have infinite metaphorical possibilities. The reason why it took me so long to work out what they were was because it seemed to me that it was a metaphor for so many different things." So it would seem that a relatively fluid access to the *unconscious* is often the wellspring of art and a certain frame of mind seems to be necessary to sustain access to unconscious resources. "My book is the means of finding out," says Tremain. "You discover what's going on as you write it," says Pullman.

Perhaps some of the excitement and aesthetic satisfaction for the reader comes from a live sense of sharing discovery not only in identification with the characters but also with the writer too, rather than passively consuming a finished product. The shiftiness, the uncertainties that all the writers allude to refer to this "journey of discovery . . . in the dark and cold" (Tremain). Peter Claire in *Music and Silence* has to play his part in the dark, a role that Waddell links with the transference object in analysis. Pullman describes how the young reader is in the dark, following Lyra's journey: "One reason that children have read it all the way through is because they can sense that they're in the position of Lyra, who doesn't fully understand everything that's going on; she herself is puzzled, tormented with fear and doubts at times, but vastly, powerfully, magnetically intrigued by this adult world that is somehow going on around her. And because the young reader trusts Lyra, and they can see that she doesn't fully understand, they're willing to follow her through and to discover what is going on. That I didn't realise either until I saw how it had happened." A similar idea comes from Byatt, whose novel under discussion is so hugely different in style from Pullman's. She also invites the reader to identify with the writer as well as the quest for meaning: "[The] text asks that you ask what is the writer doing, and why . . . That is where the centre of sympathy is, I think: the mind making sense, saying look, I think sense comes out here."

It would seem that an attitude of trusting, if circumspect, identification is central to a thoughtful experience of reading, as indeed it is to the enterprise of psychoanalysis. It is not so much an immersion of the reader in the text but more a reserved surrender to the text. One participant in the Byatt dialogue very clearly describes this as engaging in a "partial identification" in which "we are both strangers and foreigners to ourselves in the moment of reading". The writers and analysts are constantly trying to find ways of describing this paradoxical frame of mind and to tease out something of the complicated relationship of projection and identification that takes place. "The better the novel and the more complex the character, the more known to the reader it will be, the more recognisable as a "person"; and yet at the same time the more different to each it will be" is how Sodré describes it. It is a peculiar state of mind, which involves being simultaneously inside and outside, or a certain fluid movement between the two. Analysts would recognise this attitude in the reader as similar to analytic listening: it requires a similar splitting of consciousness. It is about a surrender to the emotional experience, like the surrender to the text, while at the same time holding oneself at a kind of distance in order to think about what one is experiencing and why. It is perhaps not surprising that Churcher and Pullman find themselves discussing the frame of mind that Keats named Negative Capability.

Maddox refers to the proposition that "it takes 500 Newtons to make a Shakespeare". I am very aware that, whatever similarities we may have explored between psychoanalysis and literature, it takes very many ordinary analysts to make a great novelist. We are tremendously grateful to these writers for the dialogues, for their writings, and for their generosity in allowing the conversations to be published, co-editing them, and giving their fee to support our continued work with patients.

Rose Tremain
in conversation with
Margot Waddell

Chair: Nicola Abel-Hirsch
20 October 2000

NAH: Rose Tremain's most recent novel *Music and Silence* won
the 1999 Whitbread Prize for Literature. She has published eight
novels and three collections of short stories and her work has
been translated into fifteen languages. She's a fellow of the Royal
Society of Literature, was shortlisted for the Booker Prize with
her novel *Restoration*, and has won a number of other awards.
In 1995 *Restoration* was made into a film and she's currently working on film scripts for both *Sacred Country* and *The Way I Found
Her*. Rose Tremain told me she began to write what she called
"little stories" at eleven when on her parents' divorce she was
sent with her sister to boarding school. Her early stories included
one about a boy who ran away to join a troupe of travelling
gypsies and another about a man walking through a foggy,
smoky London in search of his childhood. There was also a story
set under water with mermen and mermaids. Rose then began

to write plays and to act in them. In doing so she found her place at school. She tells me that in one play two girls decided to learn about the world by cleaning people's houses. Their employers were nasty and persecuting, and the wages poor. In another a circus troupe figured again and there were parts for everyone. This play included a dream sequence which Rose remembers little about except that it was set to Sibelius's *Finlandia*. Rose went to the Sorbonne for a year and then took up a place at the University of East Anglia. She chose East Anglia because it was a new university and because the writer Angus Wilson was there, a living writer. He read her work and asked to read her first novel. He liked it and helped her with a quote for the front cover. Much later, from 1988 to 1994, she herself taught on the MA in Creative Writing at UEA and was awarded an honorary doctorate by UEA this year. What next? As well as writing the screenplays for her two films, *Sacred Country* and *The Way I Found Her*, she also has the idea for her next book. On a recent trip to a writers' festival in New Zealand with her partner Richard Holmes, she went to South Island, a place that may be familiar to you from the film *The Piano*. Rose learnt that there had been a gold rush in this "mountainous, volcanic and difficult terrain". This provides the setting for a novel about a man in search of gold, and a woman's journey into the wilderness.

Rose will be in conversation this evening with psychoanalyst Margot Waddell. Of course Margot has read Rose's fiction but at a preliminary meeting a couple of weeks ago it became clear that Rose Tremain had read Margot's work, specifically her book *Inside Lives: Psychoanalysis and the Growth of the Personality*. Rose spoke to me of its clarity: "It has no jargon," she said, "and the case studies are marvellous." Margot Waddell studied Classics and Literature at Cambridge and wrote a PhD on the topic of "George Eliot and the Idea of Nature". She went on to train as a child psychotherapist and as a psychoanalyst. She is a consultant child psychotherapist in the Adolescent Department of the Tavistock Clinic. Two weeks ago the two of them sat on either side of a fire, clearly curious about and enjoying each other's thoughts on literature and psychoanalysis. We are lucky to have them here and I hope you will both enjoy their dialogue and later join them in conversation.

MW: I'd like to begin by putting to you some thoughts about the relationship between psychoanalysis and literature that were provoked by a comment of Johanna's, one of Kirsten's maidservants, in *Music and Silence*. At one point she says "a fable can awaken the mind to the truth of what it perceives in the daily world." That notion reminded me of a line by John Dryden, who speaks of poetry as "that which moves the sleeping images of things towards the light"—a line that I've always found to be a wonderful description of the psychoanalytic process. Reading your novels, I'm aware of just how much your way of thinking and writing has in common with a psychoanalytic way of thinking.

Perhaps, by way of introduction, I can proffer a few ideas about this common ground and see what you have to say about it. I think that, in their very different ways, both novel-writing and psychoanalytic practice are trying to find symbolic form for perceived aspects of human nature, human behaviour, the meaning of things, the value of things, and to convey those perceptions to somebody else, a reader, a patient. More specifically, it seems to me that throughout your work, from *Sadler's Birthday* to *Music and Silence*, you share with psychoanalysts an interest in the nature of identity and of personal development. I have in mind the way that you are alert to the kinds of factor, both internal and external, that lend themselves to a person's development and the kinds that arrest that development; the factors which cause a character variously to go on growing, to go mad, to shallow out, or to become merely conventional. One of the things that really strike me about your novels is that some characters do go on growing, even into old age; that, as George Eliot said, "it is never too late to become the person you might have been."

Another dimension I would like to explore is your interest in the creative process itself. Many of the novels seem to me to be about the nature of creativity, be that in music, for example, or in writing, or in architecture. In *Music and Silence* there's that extraordinary depiction of the cellar where the musicians are playing together and creating something marvellous. I take this situation to be a central metaphor of the book, perhaps a metaphor for creativity itself. But it could also be said to be a powerful representation of the psychoanalytic process too. There is a passage in *Sacred Country* where Harker, the cricket bat maker who also works away in a cellar, describes a feeling that he is the reincarnation of the lutenist from the court of Christian IV [Peter Claire in *Music and Silence*]. So it would seem that the metaphor is one that you've been mentally turning over for a long time. It's been working away somewhere, to become absolutely essential to this most recent book.

But perhaps we can begin with my asking you how you bring together historical fact (because that scene in the cellar has clearly been recorded as something that actually happened) with creativity? How do you interweave the two? It's a question of interest to psychoanalysts for it abuts on the endlessly fascinating relationship between inner and outer worlds, and between clinical facts and actual facts.

RT: I think that the idea of "working away" is very important. I was told this story about the cellar at Rosenborg about nine or ten years ago. I think it was 1990 or 1991, when I was in Denmark. It was the legend about King Christian IV, who keeps his musicians—the most creative people in Europe, the best musicians from France, Italy, Germany and Finland, a group of people who are very, very eminent—not in the state rooms but *underneath* the state rooms, in a cellar. That way, their music can drift mysteriously up. They won't be visible, but the music will come unnoticed into the upper rooms and cause wonder. I thought it presented a very powerful series of images. I saw it as a kind of split stage with the musicians—the creative people— underneath, in the cold, in the Danish winter. We know how hard it is to play a musical instrument, but imagine playing it in a cellar in Denmark in the winter! How hard it would be to keep the instruments in tune, and so on. Light was very important, the quality of light in the first two images. The musicians had a very unstable kind of light: flickering candles, and then, above, there would be a more stable, perpetual illumination of fire and oil lanterns. On one level you had people in darkness and then above them a man of power and all the appurtenances of power, up there in the light. I thought these were very beautiful images which also had infinite metaphorical possibilities. But I think the reason it took me so long to make anything coherent of them was because I felt, in a way, that their potency might be such that the story I would write would never be able to do justice to them.

MW: This idea of working away in the dark, such an intense and painful creative effort, is very suggestive for psychoanalysts as well. But there is also the striking detail that all the musicians are so different each from the other, and that their very difference is distinct from the quality of the music that they eventually produce. My own feeling is that many aspects of this novel, and of some of the others too, have to do with the process by which some way of integrating the different parts of the personality is found such that, even perhaps momentarily, there's a sense of a whole which can be communicated to others.

RT: Well, the story opens at a moment of crisis and we meet this character, Christian IV, who is, in various ways, finding his way through a maze of chaos and disorder. He is trying to re-impose some sort of harmony, to struggle through things which are disparate and split and difficult for him to something which is harmonious. And, of course, that's where music comes in. His aspirations to commission beautiful music underlie his struggle out of confusion towards something which is ordered and fruitful.

MW: Yes, and the interesting thing about the way he seeks to discover what harmony *is* comes in the person of Peter Claire and what Christian uses Peter Claire for. Because, as you make clear in so many ways, the music is to do with linking; to do with the possibility of memory based on expectation; with the sense that something can be ordered and that form can arise from chaos. The pattern by which Christian seeks to realise these creative possibilities is, in psychoanalytic terminology, what amounts to a transference relationship with Peter Claire. As the latter says, he doesn't have the faintest idea who Christian is but this figure has selected him as his angel—an angel to watch over him. Christian needs Peter to perform the function of what psycho-analysts would describe as a container for the otherwise chaotic and confused states of mind in which he finds himself. He turns to Peter in order to help himself to think, and when he's feeling most distressed and disintegrated he calls Peter up and has him play. Then he talks. Peter Claire doesn't actually say anything of enormous interest in itself, but it is as if Christian, through Peter Claire's presence and his music, is able to think for himself and, as a consequence, to resolve something for himself in the course of the book.

RT: I think Peter Claire is struggling to say things as interest-ingly as he possibly can. He is aware of this man who has given him this task. Christian has asked him to watch over him in a kind of angelic way. But of course Peter Claire is *in the dark* as to what really that task constitutes, and he's certainly in the dark about the way in which he is a kind of projection of an earlier very significant relationship that the King had in childhood and to which much guilt and sadness still adheres. So Peter Claire's task is really very difficult because he doesn't understand the parameters of what's expected of him. What can the King mean? He's asked to "watch over" him and this seems strange and undefined, yet Peter feels immediately bound to try and fulfil this role. What I was looking to establish here was the idea that the stranger who arrives in this dark kingdom is immediately entrapped. Even though Peter Claire can't formulate what the precise nature of his task is, he intuits the fact that he has to stay until that task is complete. He's in a sense a kind of prisoner.

MW: But his role is immensely helpful to Christian. Indeed, I'm very struck by the fact that in your novels there tends so often to be a central relationship of a particular kind: somebody has a "somebody else" who enables him or her to develop. I'm thinking of Mary Ward in *Sacred Country*, for example, and the very few, but significant, figures in her life. Mary is a six-year-old little girl when we first meet her. She suspects that she's really a boy, and as she becomes ever more certain, she faces the absolute destitution of her life as a girl and the attendant overwhelming loneliness. But she does have a few figures who enable her to express something of her real self: Miss McRae, the village school teacher, Harker, the cricket bat maker, Irene, a comforting soul, and Irene's daughter, Pearl, who is, like Peter Claire, described in "angelic" terms.

RT: Yes, I think that *Sacred Country* is primarily a story about emotional drought. It's a good phrase that you identify in your book *Inside Lives*. We all go through these periods of severe emotional drought, and I think Mary Ward is experiencing absolute emotional drought and would indeed perish, would die of confusion and heartbreak, were it not for one or two understanding figures who can make some attempt to identify with the problem—even though the problem is very extreme. There only needs to be one or two of these figures in any life. I think I understand, having written for more than twenty years now, that almost all my books have one or two such people, who are, of course, idealised. They're quite often male, avuncular figures—the perfect father or the perfect uncle or grandfather: the perfect understanding, intuitive, wise and faithful older person—who tries to alleviate the misery and the confusion of the younger, suffering characters. These avuncular figures have cropped up so many times that I'm starting to think of them as being a bit suspect, but there they are. They are wonderful. I wish I knew people as wonderful as them. (*laughing*)

MW: Well this is what analysts are supposed to be—except, perhaps, without the idealisation.

RT: Exactly, exactly.

MW: To change tack slightly, I'd like to explore another distinctive set of themes that thread their way through all the books, and that is the complex relationship between dreams and reality, between sanity and madness, between illusion, delusion and a sense of reality. I am, of course, particularly interested in your use of dreams. Your novels are full of them, and they would seem to be tremendously rich ways of gaining access to the internal worlds of the characters. Needless to say, psychoanalysts think about dreams all the time, but it is less usual, perhaps even risky, for novelists to draw on them.

RT: Yes, it's interesting that the analyst's reaction is "yes, dreams are fantastic, we'll pay special attention to the dreams in this book," whereas I remember my agent's response to an earlier novel which had an awful lot of dreams in it. My agent said:

"Look, get these dreams out, because nobody's going to read them, they'll just pass over onto the next bit."

I think there is a peril about dreams in literature. The prime danger is that the lay reader, if you like, will not see them as significant and will skirt over something which might be thematically important, but I'm also aware that my understanding of the power of dreams, not having had psychoanalytical training, might not be sufficient to make the dream as powerful and potent as it should be at that particular moment in the story. So in recent novels, the dreams get shorter. I only allow myself just the briefest context of the dream rather than a great rambling new story in the middle of a sequence of events.

MW: This is true, but in *Music and Silence* I think the dreams have a sort of pivotal role, especially King Christian's dream about Bror Brorson. An enormous amount hangs on how one understands these dreams. I felt it was possible that the reason the King had to resolve something about what Bror Brorson meant to him was that Bror was effectively an aspect of himself. Christian's kingship meant that he had to let go of this aspect of himself. But he couldn't it let go. He needed to hang onto it and he felt very guilty about that, and as he moved into greater and greater grandiosity and excess, he found it increasingly difficult to discern that the difference between his vision and the actual grandiose realisation of his dreams, in Fredericksborg for instance, has something huge. (He was himself a huge person.) There is a distinct blurring between grandiosity and insight. But I think that the loss of the Bror Brorson part of himself, a part which, as he experienced it, gave him life when he brought Bror Brorson back to life, is something that torments him. If one interprets the dreams from my way of thinking, one is able to get at the fact that that was part of himself as well as an external figure.

RT: Does that mean therefore that you think the symbolism of the dreams is right? There's one dream, for example, where Christian is walking towards this figure in a snowy, desolate landscape and he thinks the figure, who resembles Bror, is going to get larger and larger because he's coming towards him, and then he realises that in fact he's *walking away from him,* so he's getting smaller and smaller. Does this dream fit with your perception that for King Christian Bror Brorson is part of himself, a part that he feels is lost but actually needs to recover? Is that symbolism right? I'm not certain.

MW: Yes, that is indeed how I would see it. The point is that these sorts of dreams are so suggestive that one gets left with all manner of questions and not necessarily, thankfully, with answers. I'd like to move on now to a further point.

Many of the novels are about the respective ways in which characters are enabled to develop or, by contrast, find themselves stuck. In *The Way I Found Her*, I am interested in the portrayal of Lewis as having to live through his particular pubertal crisis more or less on his own, for his parents are, in effect, completely letting him down. He is faced with something that seems unbearably exciting in Valentina because he is involved, one would think, with her as a sort of oedipal displacement for his mother—so common in early adolescent infatuations. The book then takes off into a kind of adventure story with quite a "Boys' Own" atmosphere. At this point my own sense was that it was as if the story becomes a kind of concrete enactment of unmanageable pubertal feelings, an explosion of adolescent needs, desires, and masturbatory fantasies. It ends in catastrophe, because, as I would see it, there wasn't a sufficiently strong parental relationship available to help Lewis with so troubled and troubling a stage of development. The impression one gets is that the marriage isn't good and that Lewis is left, bereft of parental involvement, emotionally trying to survive through his capacity to draw on his own imagination. The story finally becomes a tragic playing out of Lewis's incapacity to get beyond puberty and to enter a world, perhaps of adolescence proper, which, whatever the obvious pitfalls of characteristic group life, would actually be more helpful to him. So he's just left with a mess at the end.

RT: Yes, he's left with something which you would define— your definitions of kinds of knowledge are very real to me—in terms of two types of knowledge, K knowledge and minus K. The minus K knowledge is about the accumulation of facts and material but it doesn't actually increase understanding in the person. It's towards minus K knowledge that Lewis has to come in the end, simply because life has become too painful to be borne in the unravelling of this drama. I still get very anxious letters from readers about this book saying: "I know he's not really all right at the moment we leave him because all he's got is maths, but do you think in a couple of years he'll be able to live a viable life?" I think the answer is "yes". I know psychoanalysts are quite severe about displaced knowledge, which is to do with the display of cleverness and the acquisition of facts for their own sake, but it does strike me also that in the case of an adolescent like this, for whom the most severe things have happened, there is a kind of refuge in mathematics. Lewis doesn't live with his parents any longer at the end of the book; he lives in the garden hut. It is literally just him and the maths books. That would sustain him for a period of time but then my thought about him, to reassure these anxious readers, is that his cleverness is not simply connected to figures or mathematical equations: it is a kind of *innate cleverness*. It's the kind of cleverness that can understand what is going on, on a lot of different levels.

For example, at the beginning of the book he understands very clearly the geography of Paris and the complexities of the Paris street cleaning system. It took me about 25 years to work out why all these old bits of carpet were left lying in the road and then it suddenly came to me that it is because Paris is cleaned through water, unlike London which is never cleaned through water. All these bits of carpet are deliberately put there to channel the water. It takes Lewis about five and a half minutes to work this out. It seemed to me that there would be hope for such a boy who when he's fourteen is able to work this out, as well as falling in love, as well as taking responsibility for the dog, all the kinds of things that make his world so rich in the middle of the book. He has retreated because that's all that is left for him at that moment in time. So I'm able to add, dear reader, that yes, I do think in two year's time or so, when time has passed, he will be all right.

MW: That leads me to the fact that you yourself began writing when you were obviously rather miserable and were sent off to boarding school, your parents having divorced. I think that throughout your books you bring home the role of the creative imagination in somehow holding the personality together through periods of emotional drought, whether caused by loss, separation, bereavement, unexpected change of some kind. I was touched by how [in *The Cupboard*], when eight-year-old Erica Marsh's mother dies, the little girl creates a character for herself— Claustrophobia. Claustrophobia becomes her very close friend for a year and a half or so, and obviously sustains Erica over that grief-stricken period. In so many of the books your characters draw on their imaginative capacities to tide them over periods of stress and absence—capacities perhaps rather close to your own experience.

RT: I think so. Again this is something which I find described excellently in your book when you talk, for instance, about little Mary [Lennox] in the imaginative world of *The Secret Garden*, picturing what the garden could be, and about little Sarah [Crewe] in *The Little Princess*, who is persecuted but actually finds refuge in an imaginative world. These are the kinds of transforming things which will lead these characters towards goodness, but also lead them out of spiritual aridity. Maybe we just do this automatically. In times of distress as a child, if this is your disposition, this is what you automatically do. The transforming thing might be music, or it might be painting, or whatever. I was not aware at the time what emotional function my early writing had, but the habit of replacing the actual world with a very, very vivid internal world certainly began at that time. I can certainly remember the feeling of engendering for myself a kind of refuge, a place where I could not simply feel safe—safe was too boring really—but really engaged in a new, quite energetic and positive way with a world that had nothing to do with what I was feeling deep down about my father leaving and finding myself at a boarding school. This refuge of interiority, this ability to be in an invented world, and for the invented world to have immense liveliness and substance all around me, means that there is a qualitative difference in my life between the times when I am writing and the times when I'm not writing. It's actually a very great difference. Some writers say to me: "Oh, you've finished the book, you must be feeling so relieved," but it isn't like this at all. It is much more a feeling of loss and mourning that I find at the end of a book. This parallel life, the writing life, has sustained me not just in childhood at age ten but actually through my entire existence. And I think that if for one reason or another I was not able to continue writing, I would probably become very melancholy very fast.

MW: Well, you've talked about writing as a voyage of discovery and I suppose, in a sense, it's very important that you never feel that you've arrived, nor that you've created the perfect object, because then you would no longer be moved to write. In fiction I imagine that this may be something to do with the continuing process of exploring and trying to resolve different aspects of self, life and relationships, as they get represented in all these various different characters. That urge to understand must be intrinsic to the creative process, I would have thought, just as to psychoanalysis. *Restoration* would be an obvious case in point. This novel finds a way of describing, with great ebullience, not just a particular period in history but the restoration of aspects of the personality which, in the main figure of Merivel, have been split off and lost, or divided between the King and Pearce. That process would seem to have something in common with what we're all struggling with in our different ways: seeking to restore to ourselves the lost, split off or projected bits of our personalities as we strive towards some kind of greater integration, self knowledge—obviously a lifelong process.

RT: Yes, but it's probably never as absolute or as complete as you imagine it to be. In *Restoration*, I'd created the central character—I hesitate to call him a hero because he's very unheroic really—the central character Robert Merivel, who has two defining influences upon him. On one side, there is the King, Charles II, a kind of father figure, but also a sort of god-like figure, who tugs Merivel towards the material world, towards flamboyance and libidinous behaviour. On the other side is Merivel's Quaker friend, John Pearce, who is tugging him in an absolute opposite direction. Merivel and Pearce begin as medical students together at Cambridge, and then Merivel abandons medicine and Pearce keeps urging him back, saying: "Come on, come on, this is your vocation, you were good at it, you had a feeling for it, you had a talent for it and you're just frittering away your life. Look at you, you're getting fat, you're getting stupid, you've forgotten how to think, you're disintegrating."

All of this is true. Pearce is right about his friend, and in the planning stage of the book I had the idea that by the end of the novel Merivel could actually renounce all the side of him which is in thrall to the King and become the perfectly restored good man. But in the course of writing this book, and not until maybe two thirds of the way through, I began to think: well, actually, wait a minute, I've created somebody here who is *not capable* of an absolute renunciation of this side of his nature. He has to learn to accommodate *both sides*; he has to learn not to despise himself for being what he is. So in a sense I had to reconceive my whole plan of what would happen at the end. The conclusion I reached is that the *partial* restoration of the man at the end is more truthful. So it's very interesting, I think, the way what has been very well planned out for a fiction will change—just like life changes. I hesitate to identify with the sentimental idea of the characters "taking over". It isn't exactly that they take over, but it is that they gradually acquire a kind of integrity, which the author then has to recognise and honour. By halfway through the book you hope, I guess, that all the characters, major and minor, will have that integrity. Then you just have to be able to see exactly what it is and respect it.

MW: Before we finish I want to come back to Mary Ward, who is just such an extraordinary characterisation—this growing girl who, from such a young age, believes she's a boy. I'll read a tiny bit from *Sacred Country* because I think it's so powerful. We need to bear in mind a very significant detail, namely that Mary's father, Sonny, desperately wanted a boy, repeatedly saying to his wife, Estelle: "Pray for a boy, pray for a boy." There's a sense that Mary was meant to be a boy and the fact that she was born a girl is, as she says somewhere, "like the Light Brigade, a blunder". It's as though she feels like a mistake of nature from the very beginning. Something was clearly going on in terms of the projective mode of the family, but then there's also the actual experience which is so searing. One feels that she never gets over the birth of her little brother, Timmy, that longed for boy. There's a scene early on in the novel where Mary is picking up stones on the farm with her father. She wanders off and loses sight of her parents. She's found later clinging to a tree, just standing there:

> My parents came and found me with torches. My mother was sobbing. My father picked me up and wrapped me inside his old coat that smelled of seed. He said: "Mary, why didn't you stay where you were?" I said: "My bucket is lost on the field." My father said: "Never mind about the bucket. You're the one."
>
> But when I was three, I was no longer the one. Tim was born and my father kept saying the arrival of Timmy was a miracle. I asked my mother whether I had been a miracle and she said: "Oh, men are like that, especially farmers. Pay no heed."
>
> But after Timmy came, everything changed. My mother and father used to put him between them in their sagging bed and fall towards him. When I saw this, I warned them I would kick Timmy to death; I said I would put his pod through the mangle. So my father began to think me evil. I'd go and tell him things and he'd say: "Don't talk to me, Mary. Don't you talk to me." So I stopped talking to him at all. When we went stone picking together, we would go up and down the furrows, up and down, up and down, with each of our minds locked away from the other.

I just wonder what was in your mind when you wrote so dramatically about transsexuality. The predicament I can see in some sense as the quintessence of a search for one's true identity, the expression of a feeling that something's locked up inside. Can it ever come right? But in psychological terms I'm very interested to know how you thought about Mary.

RT: Well, when I told people this was my subject, that I was writing about a transsexual experience they said: "Oh my God, this is very marginal, why are you writing about *that*?" And I said: "Well it seems to me that this kind of extreme journey— and it is extreme—is a metaphor for the kind of journey that we all make." There is a sort of self inside the self that we are, which is apparent or visible to us at certain moments only, and then it disappears again. There may be a moment, perhaps towards the end of our lives, depending on the shape of the life obviously, when we feel ourselves to be in perfect harmony with the self that we are, and indeed I suppose you might say that one of the defining goals of going into analysis is to achieve that. So I had the idea—even though it is extreme—that the transsexual experience was a fine metaphor for a universal human experience. But also, like King Christian, I'm very fond of mysteries. One thing which was revealed to me during my research for the book was the strange and mysterious epiphany which occurs—in case after case—in childhood, usually at an early age. Jan Morris, in her book *Conundrum*, describes the moment when she was lying under a grand piano, aged six, and her mother was playing Liszt. Little James Morris—as she was then—had, during those few bars of the Liszt that he was listening to, this sudden shattering, blinding conviction that he was in the wrong gender. But why? and why then? What I'm doing in *Sacred Country* is to say: "Well, this is one of the last mysterious things, so let's look at what it might be."

Science can explain so much to us about human behaviour and human knowledge and human biology, but it can't truly explain the transsexual's early epiphany. In the novel I offer many explanations, none of which is absolute. You suggested one, which was Mary Ward's sense that she should have been a boy and that her parents longed for a boy and then she wasn't it. Another one comes from the cricket bat maker who believes in reincarnation. He tells Mary that inherent in reincarnation is the role of the "angel of forgetting" who intervenes in between lives. So when you have a residual memory of a previous life, the angel of forgetting has failed in his task—and this is what's happened here, to Mary. All that's really fanciful, but I liked the idea that here is something mysterious in a world that we think we know, analyse and control. Of course we all know that the human psyche is very mysterious indeed. The book really is an exploration of that, of the mystery at the heart of things.

Audience: One of the things that I noticed in *Music and Silence* is the presence of what as a psychoanalyst I'd call a non-containing object. The two major women in the book are actually very corrupting objects in various sexually perverse ways, but not only in those terms, in a way in which they relate either to their own children or to the stepchildren. I'd like to hear what you have to say about the impact of, if you like, a corrupting object on the kind of journey that you've been talking about.

RT: Yes, this has been pointed out to me before, particularly with regard to Kirsten, the King's wife, who is almost a person-ification of what you call a corrupting object. But in fact in this narrative it's not simply Kirsten and Magdalena, I think it's also Emilia's father Johan, who's corrupting because of his dereliction of duty. So it's not simply the women. But we're talking about the 17th century here, don't forget, when women had no power, and in this narrative I wanted to show these two women collud-ing with the dictates of a male society which accords women power only through their sexuality. Kirsten is a witty woman with flair and intelligence, and she's understood how to use her beauty to get the things she wants. But what happens later in the narrative is that we see Kirsten retreating further and further inside a sort of self-delusion, so that by the end of the book she's lost touch with the real world absolutely.

And as regards Magdalena, the way I perceived the classic wicked stepmother was in terms of blood imagery. She wears red and she gives birth to the baby Ulla in the lake, and her stepson, whom she bullies, finds the placenta, the threads of the blood and placenta floating in the water. Magdalena's journey leads nowhere but to bleeding and death. But we shouldn't forget that there's also the younger woman, Emilia, who doesn't strive for power but who manages—through certain understandings and certain intuitive behaviour—to represent something powerful and non-corrupting in the book, which is the idea of goodness.

MW: I just want to add that although these characters are utterly appalling, corrupting, as has been said, it's so striking that even with what one might think of as gross pathology in psychoanalytic terms, there's still something actually quite compelling about them. There seem to be aspects of even very deprived and depraved human nature that you still write about with a degree of humour and robustness, even riotousness.

RT: Well, I do think that humour is immensely important. It's very, very important in our lives for defusing situations. It has a role in healing misunderstandings. When I used to teach on the Creative Writing MA, I would say to my students: "Remember how funny things can be dark and how dark things can be funny. Don't forget this strange juxtaposition of these two. The tragic can be comic and the comic can be tragic." So I think that I will always be attracted to the riotous or even wicked character. Even in a writer as nice as Jane Austen, the characters we remember most are the characters who scheme, not the obedient little darlings.

Audience: I wondered whether you wrote each section of your book in sequence.

RT: Yes, I wrote them sequentially. I'm always astounded by writers telling me they can write sections that come later on early, and vice versa. I find it difficult to imagine disturbing the process of the journey which, as I was saying earlier, is not just a journey for the characters, but a journey for me. When I embark on a book I don't know absolutely and precisely what it is I want to say or what it is I'm interested in until the book is done. My book is the means of finding out. So it's necessary for me to write it in sequence.

Audience: Do you enjoy turning your own novels into screenplays?

RT: Well, all I can say is that it's better than having somebody else do it. Having somebody else do it was not a very agreeable experience, because the writer lost the logic of the story and so, although I think I'm quite an accommodating person by nature, I've been unaccommodating and said that nobody will make any more movies out of my work unless I'm able to write the script. I have the illusion—it may be an illusion—that I know it better than anyone else could ever know it and so I understand what has to go into the movie and what can come out. Movie writing is simply the art of selection really, the art of stripping away. If I had to make a diagram of what happens in the writing of a novel it would show that I start with something quite small, and then the process of writing the novel is a *process of expansion.* But to write a movie from a book, the process has to go the other way. You have to get back down to this nuggety thing, strip away everything which is novelistic, everything which is meditative. This makes it sound as if the work involved might be reductive and boring, but in fact it isn't. Because new material has to come in too. This new material has to be cinematic in essence and express the heart of the book, without being the book.

Audience: I was very interested by the fact that you mentioned that you used dreams a lot in your books. I just wondered—when you use the imagery of dreams, do you have in mind for the reader to pick up certain messages and make certain interpretations from these dreams? And if so, are the images that you use based on any dreams that you've had yourself?

RT: I don't think so. As I said earlier, I think the position of a dream in a narrative is quite problematic, for reasons which I outlined, so I think one has to be very certain about what one's doing in the dreams. I would say that the dream has the same relationship to the narrative as the aria has to the opera. That is to say, with the aria, even though we sit back and say: "Here it comes, the one we all know," in fact what is spoken in the words of the aria and even the tone of the music, the mood created by the music, carries forward our understanding of what's going on. So I think the only justification for having any dream in fiction is for it to give insight into the action which carries it forward—like the aria does—so that it's not holding up the narrative.

Audience: One thing that seems to me to be extremely common in your books is the location. I wonder if you would talk a little bit about the sense you have of the places in which you put your characters and give us your thoughts about the meaning of the location. I can see why people would want to make films of the books because the location in films is so crucial, it seems to me. I was so interested to hear that it was when you got to New Zealand that another book came to mind.

RT: I think that I have two modes of relating to location. One has to do with the place where I live—Norfolk—which is not where I was brought up as a child. It's not a landscape which is innately precious to me, so I can afford to be unsentimental about it. I also think that because of the character of East Anglia, with its big skies and its wateriness and its strange quality of light, it's a landscape over which shadows pass in an infinitely astonishing way, so that it's a *changing landscape*, more so than other hilly parts of this country. In this way, it has great intensity of mood attached to it. It can sometimes be very dark and gothic, which is right for certain stories, and it can sometimes be very benign and feathery and illuminating. I think with regard to the settings in East Anglia it is some kind of relationship to this quality of light which has just stirred my imaginative response. The other mode is a search for the unfamiliar. This may be an actual landscape (Denmark, the South Island of New Zealand) but, in the historical novels, it will also be a vanished landscape, only recoverable via research and via the imagination, and I find I'm very happy in places which are partly real and partly dreamed up.

Audience: I'd like to follow up what's just been said in terms of the relationship of your historical novels to what you might call the real past. You see, there are some books which seem to me to try to tell you what it was actually like. I think Richard Holmes's book on Coleridge is like that. You can't get any nearer to what it was like being there than reading that. I think there are some novels that try quite hard to do that and I think Pat Barker's *Regeneration* really wants you to know what that was like. I have a feeling reading your historical books that you want us to get into the past and realise that it's different—and some of the parameters of the ways in which it's different your novels suggest very, very strongly—but I don't have the sense that you believe you're telling the reader that's how it was or even that that matters. So it seems to me almost as if the past constitutes an imaginary space which perhaps you believe no one is ever going to know, especially since these are very remote locations, but at any rate we can be got to think about it in a different way.

RT: I stumbled on the idea of setting a novel in history. This isn't something that I thought I was ever going to do. I wanted to write a novel about the 1980s and the way there was this sort of psychic change in the air, about materialism and the famous pronouncements of Mrs Thatcher about there being no such thing as a society and the individual moving away from communal thinking and caring and sharing—which was very much the feeling of the sixties when I was growing up—towards something much more brutal and something much more self-centred. I wanted to write about that as a sort of climate of society. But more and more time was going by and I just wasn't coming up with the engendering idea. It just wasn't there. And I realised that this had to do with the fact of contemporary life becoming harder and harder to seize in fiction because it's moving faster, changing faster than fiction can be written. So that was what propelled me towards another era, and the 17th century seemed to me to be a kind of mirror to our own times. When I look at *Restoration* now I don't think it is a perfect mirror at all, but it seemed to me perfect enough to enable me to say something about the materialism of the Thatcher years. But you're absolutely right in saying that my object, when using the 17th century, was both to locate and to disturb. First of all I wanted to put the reader into a believable 17th century, with all the noise and colour particular to it, but I wanted also to disturb the historical texture of it, so that the research—the data—was barely visible to the reader, and what emerges is an *imaginative reconstruction* of an age. As an example of what I mean: the life of King Charles II was very thoroughly researched by me, but in the book he becomes not simply the King, as known to the history books, but God / magician / father, because this is how Merivel perceives him and it's only through Merivel's eyes that he's seen. Thus, Charles II in *Restoration* is both less than the historical character and more than it. This kind of dualism with regard to the past is the right mode for the novel, I think.

Audience: You talked about having an engendering idea, a sort of nugget, and you also talked about not holding a sentimental idea of a character as taking over but that you had found yourself in situations where you deviated from your plan. What I'd like to know is, apart from research, what do you actually do before you start writing? Do you have a box file on every character? How detailed a plan do you have of where you want to get to and what you want to say? Do characters suddenly pop up halfway through that you didn't expect to have there?

RT: Yes, my planning is both meticulous and chaotic, which is perhaps the ideal way to plan something as complex as a novel. When I was planning *Restoration* I did have a box file, but my ability to file things in the right place was so bad that I kept losing things. I think there was a sort of subconscious intention here somewhere, because of course in order for things to be found, other things were found on the way. So things that I might have ignored because they'd been so meticulously filed could be rediscovered through my inability to file meticulously. So I would say—and not to draw this out too much—that it's like perhaps an athlete who does a lot of preparation for a race and then moves up to the start and doesn't absolutely know how that race is going to go. I'm not thinking of sprinters here, the novel is definitely a 1500 metre race.

MW: Sadly, we need to draw to a close. I'd just like to say that, for my part, I think that a conversation like this can be a voyage of discovery in itself, and that in talking to you and reading your novels one actually does discover things about oneself and the world—a creative process in which the writing of good novels and a good analysis could be said have something akin with one another. Thank you for so rich an evening.

A.S. Byatt
in conversation with
Ignês Sodré

Chair: Jenny Stoker
5 October 2001

JS: This evening we have with us no strangers to the forging of links between psychoanalysis and the analysis of literature. They were doing it well before this series started. We have A.S. Byatt and Ignês Sodré. A.S. Byatt is one of the country's leading novelists and critics and she also taught for many years at universities. Ignês, originally from Brazil, is a training analyst. She has been practising as a psychoanalyst in this country for twenty-five years, and for many of those years she has also had an interest in literature and psychoanalysis. The two first met in Cheltenham in 1992 to discuss *Middlemarch* at the Cheltenham Festival of Literature. Their conversation and collaboration at that time was followed a few years later by a series of conversations. They had six conversations about various authors, which were recorded and made into a book called *Imagining Characters*. Tonight they are in conversation again, and they are talking this time about A.S. Byatt's book *The Biographer's Tale*.

IS: *The Biographer's Tale* is Antonia's latest of many novels, though it will soon not be the last one any more. I am going to start by asking her to read a little bit from it, the first couple of pages, just to fill everybody in, and then we will start our conversation.

ASB: Let me begin at the beginning. I should say this is my only first person piece of writing and the narrator is male.

I made my decision, abruptly, in the middle of one of Gareth Butcher's famous theoretical seminars. He was quoting Empedocles in his plangent, airy voice. "Here sprang up many faces without necks, arms wandered without shoulders, unattached, and eyes strayed alone, in need of foreheads." He frequently quoted Empedocles, usually this passage. We were discussing, not for the first time, Lacan's theory of *morcellement*, the dismemberment of the imagined body. There were twelve postgraduates, including myself, and Professor Ormerod Goode. It was a sunny day and the windows were very dirty. I was looking at the windows, and I thought, I'm not going to go on with this any more. Just like that. It was May 8th 1994. I know that, because my mother had been buried the week before, and I'd missed the seminar on *Frankenstein*.

I don't think my mother's death had anything to do with my decision, though as I set it down, I see it might be construed that way. It's odd that I can't remember what text we were supposed to be studying on that last day. We'd been doing a lot of not-too-long texts written by women. And also quite a lot of Freud—we'd deconstructed the Wolf Man and Dora. The fact that I can't remember, though a little humiliating, is symptomatic of the "reasons" for my abrupt decision. All the seminars, in fact, had a fatal family likeness. They were repetitive in the extreme. We found the same clefts

and crevices, transgressions and disintegrations, lures and
deceptions beneath, no matter what surface we were scrying.
I thought, next we will go on to the phantasmagoria of Bosch,
and, in his incantatory way, Butcher obliged. I went on
looking at the filthy window above his head, and I thought,
I must have *things*. I know a dirty window is an ancient, well-
worn trope for intellectual dissatisfaction and scholarly
blindness. The thing is, that the thing was also there. A real,
very dirty window, shutting out the sun. A *thing*.

I was sitting next to Ormerod Goode. Ormerod Goode
and Gareth Butcher were joint Heads of Department that
year, and Goode, for reasons never made explicit, made it
his business to be present at Butcher's seminars. This attention
was not reciprocated, possibly because Goode was an Anglo-
Saxon and Ancient Norse expert, specialising in place-names.
Gareth Butcher did not like dead languages, and was not
proficient in living ones. He read his Foucault and Lacan in
translation, like his Heraclitus and his Empedocles. Ormerod
Goode contributed little to the seminars, beyond corrections
of factual inaccuracies, which he noticed even when he
appeared to be asleep. No one cared much for these
interventions. Inaccuracies can be subsumed as an inevitable
part of postmodern uncertainty, or play, one or the other
or both.

I liked sitting next to Goode—most of the other students
didn't—because he made inscrutable notes in ancient runes.
Also he drew elaborate patterns of carved, interlaced plants
and creatures—Celtic, Viking, I didn't know—occasionally
improper or obscene, always intricate. I liked the runes because I have always liked codes and secret languages,
and more simply, because I grew up on Tolkien. I suppose,
if the truth were told, I should have to confess that I ended
up as a postgraduate student of literature because of
an infantile obsession with Gandalf's Middle Earth. I did

like poetry too, and I did—in self-defence—always know
Tolkien's poems weren't the real thing. I remember discovering T.S. Eliot. And then Donne and Marvell. Long ago
and far away. I don't know, to this day, if Ormerod Goode
loved or despised Tolkien. Tolkien's people are sexless and
Goode's precisely shadowed graffiti were anything but.
Plaisir, consommation, jouissance. Glee. He was—no doubt
still is—a monumentally *larger* man. He has a round bald
cranium, round gold glasses round round, darkly brown eyes,
a round, soft mouth, several chins, a round belly carried
comfortably on pillars of legs between columnar arms. I think
of him, always, as orotund Ormerod Goode, adding more
Os to his plethora, a nice complex synaesthetic metaphor—
an accurate one—to my idea of him. Anyway, there I was,
next to him, when I made my decision, and when I took my
eyes away from the dirty glass there was his BB pencil,
hovering lazily, tracing a fig leaf, a vine, a thigh, hair, fingers,
round shiny fruit.

IS: I think we probably could just discuss what you have just
read, but I want to ask you other things first; I am sure we will
come back to this text many times during the discussion. I'd like
to start with the title: *The Biographer's Tale*, as in "The Monk's
Tale" or "The Nun's Tale". The biographer is writing a tale,
which is also your story about a biographer, who is the narrator;
he is writing a biography of another biographer, a biographer
who, he discovers, tells tales. So it's a very complicated title. You
quote Goethe: "These similitudes are charming and entertaining,
and who does not enjoy playing with analogies?" And, of course,
this is very much also what the book is about. It is a comic novel:
most of it is extremely funny. It is also about very serious things,
about literature and writing. It is about the most important
things for psychoanalysis as well, about truth and fiction and
reality. And it is written like a puzzle, something that constantly

makes the reader stop and do a sort of mental acrobatic act. The way it is written is fascinating and I wonder if you could say something about that.

ASB: Yes, like most of my writing its genesis is very old. I had a note in my notebooks, which kept coming back for many years, saying, write the biography of the biographer. And I was always going to write a story called "The Biography of the Biographer". It only got called *The Biographer's Tale* when it began to acquire all this peculiar Chaucerian narrative, rather to my surprise. Rather like *Possession*, it began as a kind of rather cobwebby, mirrory image. And I had the idea of a man whose life was no life, because it was only lived through other people's lives, sitting in the British Library reading other people's letters, constructing other people's stories, simply not living—a rather Henry James-like character, like Henry James's story *The Beast in the Jungle* about a man who was perpetually expecting a really great event—and the great event was that he was the unique man to whom *nothing happened*. It was going to be like that, but when I started writing it, it seemed very necessary that it should be very artificial because it was about the unknowability of human beings. That's why it became a game. It's something to do with liking puzzles and labyrinths and mirrors, which are an image for some part of our own nature, which we can't know.

And also, I should like to say that I felt I had betrayed myself when I wrote *Possession*, because *Possession* was meant to be a novel about how biographers can't find out the really important things about people. One of the reviewers said "this is a novel about how biography reveals truths that literary critics can't reveal," and I saw to my horror that this was partly true. I had cheated myself of the distress I feel about biographers. So I thought this time I would do it properly, and present a biographer with an impossible problem. And even in the little I read out there are several things which simply end up against brick walls.

Phineas doesn't know, ever, what happened to Goode. He never really tells you what happened to his mother, and he never really tells you what she was like. That's what you know about her: that she was dead. And it goes on rather like that. It is, I suppose, an irritating book.

IS: It is, of course, terribly provocative to the reader, because you have to keep doing these mental acrobatics; but what you just said about your hero and how much he, like the reader, doesn't know, reminded me that what happens is that the narrator, Phineas Nanson, becomes a biographer because Ormerod Goode, whom he is talking about in the passage you just read, makes him a biographer; he does so by suggesting that he reads the most wonderful biography ever written, by somebody called . . . is it pronounced Scholes?

ASB: Scholes Destry-Scholes. After the footballer. There is an English footballer called Paul Scholes and that's how I know it's pronounced Scholes.

IS: I was wondering if the name was meant to suggest "scholar" . . . For a long time I also thought it was pronounced "shoals"; so I imagined all these little fish . . .

ASB: Yes I know, you sent me an email and a most wonderful piece of prose about a shoal of small fish scattering.

IS: Well, so much of the novel is about fragmentation and mosaic building; I think this is why I thought of "shoals". Obviously, this is my own free association to this aspect of the novel . . .

ASB: It is a novel about free association.

IS: It is that as well. The thing is, it stirs up your curiosity
the whole time; it proceeds like an ordinary novel, a very
good novel, a comic novel, with characters and plot, and you read
on and feel caught up in it . . . And then suddenly you have all
these other strange bits in the middle, interrupting the flow of
the story, and you, the reader, have to stop and try to understand;
because you, the author, don't immediately allow the reader to
know exactly where they belong, to what level of the narrative,
to which of the various plots-within-plots. I remember the point
where Phineas decides to give up writing for good because
he is completely lost, he does not understand who Destry-Scholes
is and what exactly he is up to: suddenly there is, from the
narrator's point of view, a complete opacity. He thinks Ormerod
Goode thinks he is a failure. He is leaving the room thinking:
"I am a failure" and Ormerod Goode says to him: "There is
something very shifty about the manuscript"—and he realises
that the confusion is external to him, it belongs within the text;
and the moment he hears that, he is back on track, isn't he? And
at that point, as the reader of the novel, I wanted to stop you, the
author, and say: "There *is* something a bit shifty about all this,
about the way the novel is written, what is it?" So this both drives
the reader on and simultaneously makes him step back and
rethink his position in relation to the text.

ASB: Yes, the shiftiness is, at a serious level, to do with the
impossibility of the truth. Phineas finds almost no evidence
because he is a useless biographer, because he is actually a
person rather like myself, incapable of asking people personal
questions. So he goes and stands outsides Scholes Destry-
Scholes's house for some time, the house where Scholes was
born, and then he just goes home again. But he does manage to
find three unfinished narratives by Destry-Scholes: a biography
of Ibsen, a biography of Sir Francis Galton and a biography of

Linnaeus, the taxonomer. He discovers that these three documents are shifty in the sense that they transmute from historical fact into something that continues to look like a document with evidence but becomes fiction. I myself partly thought of this because I started reading biographies of Linnaeus and discovered that Linnaeus wrote an autobiographical account of his travels through Lapland, a large part of which scholars slowly began to realise were lies, because he couldn't possibly have covered those distances in those days. He said he went up various mountains, and he said he went to see the maelstrom, and he simply didn't. And in a sense I cheated because I included and then embroidered upon Linnaeus's real lies, and then I invented a huge lie that Scholes Destry-Scholes had told about Galton, who travelled in Namibia as a very young man. He was heading towards a particular lake, which he in fact never managed to visit. He never got there as there was a drought and nobody would take him. But Scholes Destry-Scholes invents his visit to the lake, and gives an account of the horrible things he discovers on the shore. And then he finds a small play about an event in Ibsen's life. Ibsen had an illegitimate son when he was sixteen, who came to look very like him. Ibsen's friends had the idea of putting this son in Ibsen's clothes, in the chair, in the café to which Ibsen, like clockwork, went every day, to see what Ibsen would do when he came and found himself sitting in the chair. So far this is true. The friends and the son got cold feet and gave up. But I invented and dramatised this encounter.

The book is really about the creative imagination, filling in the gaps in people's lives that you don't know. But it also shows you that there are real gaps that you can't fill in—which is why it is irritating. But people are irritating.

IS: But also, when you, the reader, stop to think, you start asking all kinds of ridiculous questions like: "Is this bit written by

Scholes Destry-Scholes or is it written by A.S. Byatt?" And it takes you a few seconds to be jolted back into common sense: "Oh, of course it is all written by A.S. Byatt," which you had momentarily forgotten. I caught myself reading terribly carefully, trying to decide which bits Antonia had written, and which bits Scholes Destry-Scholes had written; with the added complication, of course, that the fictional characters are writing about real people. So it's terribly interesting and confusing.

ASB: Some of it I know I am a bit worried about because some, quite a lot, of the real people are made up of straight quotation. It's a kind of patchwork of real things these real people really said. At the time it was perfectly clear to me which bits were written by me and which bits were written by them, but of course as you get further away from it, you begin to wonder if you wrote this or if they did, and then you—then the scholarly side of me— begins to think that the whole book is an illegitimate exercise. But it is nevertheless an example of a mental process which we all go through.

IS: But it is also *about* that process. It's about the differentia- tion, or lack of it, between fantasy and fiction and truth; the differentiation between a lie and a fantasy, between the different meanings of what is real and what is unreal. So that when I say it is about the most serious things it could possibly be about, it certainly is that. It's odd when you start to think about these serious matters, things which for us analysts are terribly important, in the middle of a very funny novel where hilarious things are happening. But there is something else which I think is part of this discussion, which is the way this may link with the question of fantasy and creativity. Take, for instance, the maelstrom, which is one of your central stories. Linnaeus said he went to the maelstrom but he didn't really, so this was a lie

—or could we call this fantasising or daydreaming? If he was writing fiction, he would be being creative, he wouldn't be a liar. In your story, the "real" Scholes Destry-Scholes dies in the maelstrom . . .

ASB: Probably.

IS: Or maybe not. In fact, I phoned Antonia and said: "Did he die in the maelstrom?" and she said: "I don't know, actually." I think the fact that he is the only character in the novel who remains completely opaque throughout must be important. The way you arranged the quotations and the way you intermingle them with other things may not give us a complete picture of Linnaeus, but it gives us a lot about him; but Scholes Destry-Scholes remains opaque. In the Galton narrative there is a lot about circulation of the blood, and one has the feeling that in the writing of a biography it is the biographer's own blood which is transfused into the corpse of the subject being written about. There is a very interesting story about transfusion in the book, a real story, about Galton and Darwin and the rabbits.

ASB: Oh yes.

IS: Do you want to tell us that story?

ASB: Yes. They had a sort of argument because Galton was trying to prove that Darwin's hereditary "gemmules" were carried in the blood. So he got different coloured rabbits and transfused one with the blood of the other rabbit, knowing nothing, of course, about blood groups because nothing was known, and the rabbits kept dying and Darwin kept sending him more experimental rabbits. Galton wrote all this up and Darwin disowned him and said that his theory had never been like that and that Francis Galton was misquoting.

IS: But this is pertinent to the whole question of writing: the writer's mental "blood"—thoughts, memories, fantasies, fragments of experience—is transfused into the subject, real or fictional.

ASB: Yes, in the sense that it was interchangeable, that people could be changed. I had a sense all the way through writing it that in some way all the characters are the same character. There is a sense in which at one level all human beings have the same characteristics. One of the things I did was to read Ibsen, Linnaeus and Galton. I just read everything I could get and picked out at random any quotations that could be put into a pattern. So I had a whole series of rather beautifully related quotations on drowning, which are not really related at all except that Ibsen, Linnaeus and Galton all talked about drowning. And I felt that that was very poetic and very moving and at the same time very particular to each of them. Linnaeus lost his very best friend by drowning. They sat discussing the taxonomy of fish in Leiden one night until very late at night and then his friend walked home and drowned in a canal. And Linnaeus had to identify the body the next day. They were twenty-five. And there is an amazing account by Galton, at about the same age, of falling off a paddle steamer at Putney and going under the paddle and the boatman refusing to pick him out of the water because he looked so horrible. He says: "It is very interesting, I can now tell you, dear mother, that when you are dying it is all perfectly all right, you feel quite calm." And that goes next to various very powerful Norwegian images about drowning out of Ibsen. It is an arbitrary game but it somehow produces something human and poetic.

IS: I thought that the maelstrom, to which these stories of drowning are connected, was a very powerful image. I reread Edgar Allen Poe's *A Descent into the Maelstrom,* and thought about this experience of going into the deep, somewhere where you may or may not perish, where things fragment; perhaps all kinds of mental content and knowledge, bits of information, of cultural experience, have to fragment in your mind so they can then be put together in a different, new way when you are constructing a work of art. There is a central metaphor in your book about fragmentation and putting together in new forms, like creating a mosaic; perhaps one of the reasons why you chose the maelstrom as a central symbol is that in the Poe story the boat goes down, deeper and deeper, and one of the brothers dies and the other one survives; he survives because he notices that amongst all the objects that are going down with them, there are some with cylindrical shapes which don't go all the way to the bottom, they come back and move towards the surface of the water. He lashes himself to a barrel and saves himself. I wondered if this could be a metaphor for creativity: the artist going all the way to the depths, and coming up again: alive to tell the tale, literally. But also I thought that Poe's character has the mind of a scientist, and you love scientists ... had you thought of that?

ASB: I hadn't thought of it in the way you said it, no. But I did like him for that reason, and it's also very typical of Edgar Allan Poe that he can write gothic terror, but he's also got this precise scientific mechanical mind. In the Poe story there are two, there are doubles. All the way through this novel there are doubles. There is the one that survives and the one that doesn't and people are mirrors of other people. People are never in love with one woman, they are always in love with two women. In the Poe story there is one that went down and one that came up. I have to say that I didn't know the Poe story when I had the idea of the maelstrom. I went and read it and then I snitched a bit of it and quoted it in amongst Destry-Scholes's account of going down the maelstrom. My German translator rang me up and said:

"I am right aren't I, you didn't write this bit, this bit is Edgar Allan Poe." So I said: "Yes." I thought: "She will do a good translation." She said: "The sentence lengths are wrong," which showed what a good ear she has.

IS: You chose Galton and Linnaeus because you are interested in natural sciences, like in your choice for your hero in *Angels and Insects*. In the "Insect" novella you said you modelled your scientist on Lydgate. You are very interested in the scientific mind and the creativity in the scientific mind.

ASB: I think that one of the reasons for that might not strike you professionally, but does come out of the bit that I just read. When I was a girl, I was obsessively literary. Those who were good at literature didn't do science. We felt it was organising and dull and static, and that some kind of creative organic life was in art and literature. And something awful, in my view, has happened. I'll just throw this out provocatively: I agree with Phineas that something awful has happened to the study of literature in recent years. It has become pseudo-scientific, and I have taken to reading real science as a kind of cure for that, to see people really thinking—as Phineas says in that bit I read out—about *things*, real things and not imaginary, constructed, over-related things. And I think this is intensely liberating, I find it exciting in a way I used to find art exciting. You've said several times that this is a work of art that is like a mosaic. I was brought up to believe that a work of art should be like an organic body, it should grow out of its own nature, like a tree or a plant, or an animal. I now think there are good works of art that are pieced together, where the pieces can still be seen to be pieces, like experimental science, where you are working with things you *have to get right*, or like maths. There is a lot of early American modernism which is to do with juxtaposition rather than a kind of organic fusion. So even in the mosaic making there is a kind of respect, or at least it goes in my mind with a respect, for science. The two scientists I chose were both great systematisers: Linnaeus inventing his taxonomy and Galton inventing statistics and all sorts of other things. People tend to think of him as the eugenicist. But in fact he invented the weather balloon, he invented all sorts of things besides, he invented the distribution from the mean as well as inventing eugenics. He was a most amazing man whose mind worked laterally in leaps and bounds. I like looking at that kind of mind. Yes, it's exciting.

IS: You are describing the organic growth of a work of art, which is different from the putting together of a mosaic, and I think that this novel is both; the "novel" part of your novel does develop organically. The characters develop as personalities, the plot develops from within itself; and then you have all the metaphors of the "things" that are collected by the characters, the cards and the marbles, and your own collection of real facts and true quotations interspersed within the text of the "novel". It is interesting that things come in twos in dramatic ways: as in one person dies and one lives. But also everything comes in twos because this is a comic novel, and everything is allowed. You have two denouements, two separate happy endings with two different women. They are allowed to coexist, because this is not a tragedy, it is a comedy.

ASB: When we wrote *Imagining Characters*, we knew we were transgressing in writing literary criticism about characters in books as though they were real people, because we had both been taught from different angles, professionally, you mustn't do that. And we both believe very strongly that when you are reading a novel it's impossible not to do that. Therefore the process of reading as though the character in the book was a real person must be allowed for by anybody studying the nature of reading, so we just did it. But when Ignês read *The Biographer's Tale*, she sent me an email saying: "If one of those women found out about the other one, what would Phineas do?" And I said this is a very artificial fiction and it *ends there.*

IS: Phineas the student of literature hates this question of identification with the characters; he complains about people identifying with the characters in literary texts. He says: "It is a disgusting *skinned* thing," meaning there is too much skin involved, or maybe not enough skin, too much rawness. This is a comic novel and therefore you are allowed to have two different endings, and you look at this from the outside. But the moment the characters feel real, you, the reader, do identify with them and worry about them: "Oh my God, they are going to be terribly jealous!"

ASB: Well, it is an experiment to prove that this always happens. You know that this is my deep belief, that the moment you start telling a story, you start caring about the characters, and no matter how clever or postmodern the novelist is, the moment the story starts moving as a tale, you start responding to the characters as people. And this is good, and it's human, and it's like life.

IS: And it is certainly very much part of the pleasure of reading that you can go emotionally into that world.

ASB: I got very fond of Phineas, because I didn't really know him. He was a hypothesis when I started with him. I only knew that he was very, very small really and didn't want to be a postmodernist, poststructuralist graduate student, with which I had great sympathy. But he is not my generation and he is not my sex and I sort of had to . . . I kept wondering what he would do next, and then I observed it as it were, so in some ways it was much more primitive than if I were writing about somebody more like myself. He just did his things and then I sort of looked at them a bit more and thought: "Yes, that's how it was."

IS: When you say he was very small, you mean he was feasibly, realistically small. But I also thought that you were making him a bit like a fairytale character. I think someone who is very, very small, especially a man, and who is completely happy about it is probably more like a fairytale character who knows there are magical advantages to being small. He says he's very nimble and he knows that he can do all kinds of things that big people can't do.

ASB: Yes, I had thought of him as Tom Thumb. He is a kind of Tom Thumb person. I have also thought that most men I know who are very small have, at one stage or another, wished they weren't, so I wanted it to be an advantage to him to be very small, rather than not being. And also he needed to be called Nanson.

JS: On that note we should, rather reluctantly, because it has been so enjoyable listening to you both, open up the conversation to the audience.

Audience: Harking back, way back in your history, what do you suppose were the influences that led you to become a successful and distinguished fictionalist?

ASB: There were the Brothers Grimm, Sir Walter Scott, Alexandre Dumas, and there was having asthma, and sitting in bed with books that were more real than the outside world. It really was a question of living in a phantasmagoria as a child, in which life in books was much better than life outside books. And I have always been trying to get back there. The reason I write complicated books is because I was academically quite good, so I kept getting trapped into studying books as well as writing books. But it was my first real pleasure, reading, which is why I always get troubled if people write reviews of my books saying this is simply dry and papery because it's just bookish. I always had the sense that perhaps I did live in a phantasmagoria, but it was what I *lived* in. The other thing is that my generation's childhoods on the whole were extremely boring. I do not think the present generation is haunted by boredom as we were. I think it has other anxieties, and other problems, but it doesn't have to fill them up with very long books and so, anyway, that's where I think it came from.

Audience: I just want to ask you a question in relation to what you take up in your book about the matter of facts, and the facts that are related to "things", the pleasure of having something that is sort of a "thing" for a fact. Since we are discussing the matter of biography, what do you think about the whole problem in biography being the limitations of knowledge, or what the biographer projects into the subject that he is studying, and so on? And what about the nature of certain fundamental facts that really are the case about someone? For instance, when Beckett moved from Ireland and presumably from his mother and began life again in France and adopted a new, as it were, mother tongue, he became this extraordinary sort of creative force in his own area. That seems to be like a fact in a way about the nature of this man. I wonder whether you could say something more about that whole issue in contrast to the imagined side that you were describing before.

ASB: I think all biographies—well, except dreadful ones—contain facts of that kind. Phineas distinguishes between "things" and facts, and this is why he finds Destry-Scholes's collection of little hard glass marbles, which are "things". A fact comes from the Latin "factum" which means it *was made*. That is, a fact in a narrative is something that someone has constructed, but it may nevertheless be true. It is not the same as a "thing" which sits about and is solid to touch. And one of the things that endlessly fascinate me is the way in which a fact, in a fiction, can slide into a fiction, or a fact in a history can slide into a fictive statement. I have been doing a lot of work in the last few weeks, at one in the morning, because I really ought to be doing something else, on people in the 1880s, round about the Bloomsbury group, and I know quite a lot of facts about David Garnett, such as that he married Angelica, the daughter of Vanessa Bell. I have no idea what he is like because every biography I've read has got a different angle on him. And then I read his book *Lady into Fox* which is also a "fact". The book exists, it's a metaphor of a woman suddenly one morning being transmuted into a vixen. In a sense I think that's more a truth about David Garnett than any of the facts about who he went to bed with or who he married. But some of them are facts and some of them are just what the biographer thinks *probably* happened. And it's all this shading which makes you very, very anxious that you get to the point that Ignês was making: when does the biographer's blood start running through the veins of the imaginary Garnett? The imaginary Garnett might be a real one, or he might be a completely fictitious one at this point. It is a very, very dangerous form and it frightens me to death. Somebody sent me three quotations from a biography they had written of somebody else that were of no real importance, that were about my life. They were all untrue, in my view, but they were "facts" they wanted to check.

Audience: The question I want to ask is: what exactly are the differences or the similarities between the way we know a character in a novel and the way we know a person in real life?

ASB: This is one of the most beautiful and most fascinating problems for any writer inventing a person, or any person reading. I think the reason I like novels is because they are private. You read a novel by yourself, to yourself, with yourself, and in fact about yourself. And somebody has written this novel not for you personally, because they don't know you, but for some imaginary other persons who will reconstruct these people in their heads. If there is one thing I know both as a writer and as a teacher, it's that every reader imagines the characters slightly differently. You can play a psychological game with the appearance of a person, and this works even more with the psychology of a person. You can say: "Imagine a woman sitting in a chair." You can make her about thirty-five and put her in a green dress. You can make her breasts be slightly sticking out above the edge of her garment. You can put a lot of bright red lipstick on her and give her big cheeks, and still everyone in the room will see a different person. None of you will be seeing the same woman in the same chair. And this also applies to the construction of the inner life of a person, though obviously slightly less. If you meet people, you know the externals fairly well, you can look at their clothes and their shoes, and you listen to what they say, and you try and piece them together. In most novels what you really *know* about important characters is the thought process, but even so every reader knows something different, and I like the sense of the endlessness of it. I like the sense that all of us have to get to know Dorothea in *Middlemarch* and we all know a slightly different person, and this is, of course, true of knowing your friends and relations too. And the older I get the more true it seems to be of my friends and relations, whereas I know Dorothea quite well because I have been thinking about her for years.

IS: I suppose it's true that the better the novel and the more complex the character, the more known to the reader it will be, the more recognisable as a "person"; and yet at the same time, of course, the more different each reader's imaginary picture will be.

ASB: Because most of it is projection, of course. You can't put yourself into Dorothea if you are a really good reader, because you "know" that she really exists.

IS: On the other hand, because the feelings and thoughts of the character seem real, I also have more of a chance of identifying with her. So both are true: in imagining a complex character there's projection but also more identification, because the truer it is, the closer to human nature it is.

ASB: That's very interesting.

Audience: You mentioned the double earlier and I happen just to have read this astonishing book by James Hogg, *Memoirs and Confessions of a Justified Sinner*, and I am thinking also of a story like *The Secret Sharer* by Conrad. I wonder if we don't think of the double as a conceit. I am sure you don't just think of it as that, but how do you see this arising in literature? I think it was in the last century that this whole theme of the double arose. Therapy proposes the idea that a person may have sub-personalities, but I don't think the double is just quite as simple as that. I'd love you to say something about how you see the double in literature.

ASB: Partly I can't answer that because the novel I have just finished has a pair of identical twins in it, and a Manichean cult, and the Manichean religion depends on the idea that everybody has a heavenly twin who shows them the path of light that is in them. And so I am sort of blocked because I am exhausted by doing that, and the whole novel is full of mirrors. Otto Rank, was it, who wrote a book called *The Double*, which has a footnote about a rich Englishman whose mistress betrayed him, so he locked her up naked in a room of mirrors so she could see how awful she was, and she went mad. This is just a footnote, and he actually dates it through a newspaper, in 1922, I think. It's also to do with the shadow. Your shadow is different from your mirror image, which is different again from somebody genetically related to you who isn't like you. I have started thinking about what it must have been like before most people saw mirrors. There is a most wonderful essay in Alberto Manguel's new book called *Reading Pictures* about the Philostratos painting of the soldier who is dying, who sees his own image in his shield reflected. Manguel makes the point that it is probably the first time since there were mirrors that this man had actually seen this person that wasn't himself, who was in the process of dying. It is an incredibly rich subject.

Audience: I was struck in listening to the immediate response to your presentation, if you will, or conversation, in that there is a question of fact. How can we distinguish fact from not fact, as if we were looking for some kind of peg in the ground to enable us to contain our anxiety without being cast adrift on to the winds of our own free associations. It occurred to me that perhaps another peg would be language. And I noticed the little side-swipe at the French and the postmodernists, Lacan and so on. It occurred to me that in language there is a question of how we translate from one language to another, either from within an experience of an individual subject or across different languages. And the word "Nachträglichkeit" occurred to me, which is notoriously difficult to translate from German into English, let alone French. But it is probably germane to this question of trying to think about what is truth, and, of course, it takes us to the notion of desire. This is where I thought perhaps there is a link between the endeavour of the biographer and the endeavour of the analyst, in the sense that it is always trying to discover something about the other's desire, but it's always being influenced by one's own desire. And so I found myself wondering what you think about how when you write someone is inevitably encountering your own desire. And about how every reader sees a slightly different character, that is, every reader encounters their own desire, at some level.

ASB: I think Ignês should speak about this, but there is just one thing I want to say, which is that I have thought about this quite a lot myself, and I know that the thing I love most is language. I need to be making strings of language, the way I need to eat, or sleep, or have people I love around me. I need to be actually producing at the end of my fingers these words, and if the sentence feels a good shape, or if a metaphor appears, this is the most pleasurable thing. And one of the nice things about getting old and getting technically slightly more proficient is that it gets to be less and less anxious-making and more and more pleasurable. But I think Ignês should also speak about desire and language.

IS: Yes, well, I don't know if I can answer the question, if I understood it, but I think probably from the point of view of the reader, a reader reading a great novel, and being fully involved in it, the novel will satisfy, at different levels, wishes and fantasies and desires, from the most basic to do with identification and feeling involved in the plot and wanting whatever it is you think the characters want, to something much more profound to do with the wish for knowledge, the wish for understanding, the very deep desire to know more about minds. In that sense the reader and the psychoanalyst aren't a million miles away from each other. There is the patient's narrative, and there is a narrative created in your mind about the patient; there is a narrative in fiction, which ultimately, if it's a good book and truthful in terms of psychic reality, draws you in because of your wish to know more; as in analysis, it may also help you fight your wish not to know. I don't know about après-coup ["Nachträglichkeit"] in this context. I suppose every involvement with anything in which you engage your full self does transform something in your mind. Presumably every deeply meaningful experience reconstructs something, and this includes changing the "past" in your inner world. Somebody asked me once about *Middlemarch*: "Should Gwendolen Harleth, who in *Daniel Deronda* starts a process of psychological growth from narcissism to a more mature way of understanding herself, read *Middlemarch*? Would it be good for her development to read *Middlemarch*?" I think that's an excellent question because it implies that through reading you can actually rethink things and be transformed, whilst simultaneously, through the idea of a character in a book reading another book by the same author, containing a sense of the different dimensions of what is fictional "truth".

ASB: And if you are writing a fiction, you get brought up by the idea: this isn't true, this isn't right, and what sort of truth is it that it isn't, as it's all a fiction anyway? That's also something: it's not necessarily to do with your own life or even, I think, the structure of your own self, but with your sense of the world as it is. I try increasingly *not to write* things that aren't true, as they mess up the whole novel. I try to stop before I've written them, because if you write something that isn't true, you have to stop for two or three weeks and put it away until you've forgotten it, and then write it right. That must be very like constructing yourself in an analysis. You know, if you get it wrong it's really quite bad.

Audience: One of the things I want to ask about and get a comment on from both of you is the way the biographer constructs himself in the process of writing the biography, because Phineas is somebody you do get to know quite well in the book and he does develop and change. It seemed to me that you could think of the parallels with self-analysis in a sense, because in the process of analysing a patient we learn quite a lot about ourselves as well.

ASB: We've talked a lot about this area between the two people, between the analyst and the patient, that they share, and I think that is also very true about the area between the reader and the writer, but then there is also the character sitting in.

IS: Each person's analysis is full of "characters", the real, external characters and the internal objects as well, so there is a very populated world between the two people in the room. In this sense, it is very much like the one between the writer and the reader.

ASB: It is a process of discovering, I suppose, this novel is about . . . anybody can invent, I guess a bad analyst can invent a patient, or can invent what has happened to a patient, and I have never had the courage to write a story about being invented by somebody who knows more than you do about yourself. Then you end up with something like the *Confessions of a Justified Sinner*, or that kind of atmosphere. Phineas in fact stops writing when he realises he is writing autobiography, because he doesn't like that either. He says: "I have just reached the point where I am writing that terrible cliché, the novel about the creation of a writer, so I am going to stop," and he goes off to be an ecologist—which is facts and things.

IS: Can I read one line, whilst we wait for another question, from your essay *The Greatest Story Ever Told*? I just happened to see this sentence last night, which I hadn't noticed when I've read it before, and I thought, this is really interesting about the nature of how when one reads one imagines not just the characters but also their writers. You said: "Storytellers like Calvino and

Scheherazade can offer readers and listeners an infinity of *incipits*, an illusion of inexhaustibility." Now what interests me, second time round, is that Calvino and Scheherazade don't entirely belong together, so why put them in the same universe? It reminded me of when somebody asks me who was the greatest influence on my deciding to be an analyst, I always want to answer "Sigmund Freud and Sherlock Holmes," because I feel they are the same character in my mind, one evolved into the other, and they feel, at that moment, equally real; they are not, obviously, and yet internally they are.

ASB: I think this is one of the dangers of biography again, because it assumes they are equally real. I think Calvino saw himself, in a way, as being like Scheherazade and in the novel *If on a Winter's Night a Traveller* he has a persona who is a novelist who keeps finding all these beginnings and can't find any endings, and finds himself endlessly reading another novel. You couldn't say George Eliot was Scheherazade with the same propriety. Calvino sort of slips away.

IS: This is something to do with the reader's internal relationship with the storyteller, which very much informs the sense that, though as you say writers are not writing for you in particular because they are writing for their own imaginary reader, the reader often feels that the writer is present as a person, that he has a relationship with him and that he writes especially for him. In that sense Calvino and Scheherazade are the same person and belong together because they are both storytellers, even if one is a fictional one. The "author" in one's mind is an amalgamation of several people—in your inner world giving you this wonderful thing, opening the door to some wonderful new world.

ASB: Yes they do, and I was thinking as you were speaking that Scheherazade is for me the archetypal storyteller, but she is also an archetypical novelist in a way, because her stories are told privately to an audience of two people in bed at night. She is not the same figure as a public storyteller addressing an audience.

IS: And she is a character in the story as well.

ASB: Yes she is, and you relate to her both as a character and as the person conducting the stories. There is this peculiar aesthetic pleasure about the changing of depth that you have just described when you realise that. Lawrence Durrell once did something I don't think he ever got enough credit for, which was inventing a novelist who was writing a novel about a character and then making that novelist walk into that character in the street. And then he just goes on telling the story as if both these people were now in the same story. They start acting together. It was an incredibly brave thing to do as a bit of narrative effort, and nobody ever seemed to notice it. I puzzle and puzzle about it: it's like a Moebius strip, because I remember him giving an interview and saying it was rather a daring thing to do, but I've never seen it remarked upon as a technical oddity. But it's more than that. It's one of the Avignon Quintet. It's quite early on, and the story keeps dropping into different levels of reality, and of course his pull is exactly the psychological desire that you were speaking of, to treat everybody as real within it.

Audience: I'm thinking about what has been said about immersing oneself in a text, actually believing in it, being at one with it, which strikes me as not exactly what happens. I don't think we actually do buy completely into what the writer is saying, and what I particularly like about A.S. Byatt's work is that in a sense it is slightly resistant. I think one of the problems we have in the modern world is that we are still governed by St Augustine's theory of healing, which is that every part must be exactly the same as the whole, and that if it is not exactly like the whole it's wrong, it shouldn't be there. Now it strikes me that when we are reading, what we engage in is partly identification, but also that we are kind of both strangers and foreigners to ourselves in the moment of reading. That is why I was fascinated by what you were saying, Antonia, about the notion of words which are pieced together, because in that kind of collage what's happened is that it allows the reader space to speculate for themselves, and not purely read. It is in a sense, therefore, a kind of co-creation which is not I think purely an issue of encountering one's own desire, but actually of constructing oneself, which I think is somewhat different. I just wonder what you think about that.

ASB: As you were speaking I thought when you are writing you do actually often . . . it's interesting I am using the second person . . . I, the writer . . . now we have the first person and the third person . . . we all stand back from time to time and say: "It's interesting what she's doing there, she is doing that for this reason." And of course that might or might not get into the text. You know, you might comment on the fact that there is a stranger and a foreigner; equally there is a time when you are the reader of your own work, when you are trying to pick it all up in order to continue with the knitting, to see where you had got to in the pattern. In that sense it's always provisional, it's always the collage, you are always outside it and always inside it. When I was taught literary criticism when I was young, one had—I didn't think of it as Augustinian—but one had this sense of the harmony of the whole. And the French, of course, have it very badly, because they have much more stringent rules than the British have ever had about the shape of a thing and the rules of the structuring of a thing, and how you mustn't break these rules. That's two remarks: one about the writer being outside the writer's text and observing him or herself, and the other is about the completeness and harmony of the text, but I think there is a certain transgressive pleasure about introducing different levels of reality, or different tones of voice, or different kinds of narrative, or different angles on where you thought you were coming from. Like the Durrell in a way. What do you think?

IS: I think that perhaps it is important to remember that there are always gaps that are filled in by the reader's imagination, and the separateness of each reader; but there is something very particular in this text that constantly makes you step out and rethink and reconstruct something in a more active way.

ASB: I think one could go a bit further and say that this text actually asks you to think about the writer, precisely because it doesn't. It asks that you ask what the writer is doing, and why, and in that sense it is a kind of intellectual game that I, or she, is asking you to play with me. But it is more than a game, as Ignês said. That is where the centre of sympathy is, I think: the mind making sense, saying look, I think sense comes out here, what do you think?

IS: I was thinking about *Middlemarch* again and the chapter that starts with "Dorothea ... But why always Dorothea?" George Eliot does make you ask that question, she makes the reader step out and rethink not just what the novelist is doing, but quite actively about the whole question of the centrality of self.

ASB: Indeed, and there's the rhetorical form of that ... I mean, who is saying "Why always Dorothea?" and to whom is that person saying it? Is it George Eliot saying it to George Eliot, or is it George Eliot wagging her finger at Dorothea, or is it ... ? One of the things I love is the narrative voice in *Middlemarch* which sometimes says "I think" and sometimes says "we think".

When it says "we think" it's making general observations about human nature, and it would like its reader to be part of this first person plural, which is a very rare thing to find in a novel actually.

Audience: I have got a question about gaps too, but from a rather different angle. You talked fascinatingly about why you like to write about science as creative, and of course that's a major theme of *The Biographer's Tale*. It struck me, as you said that, that there is a potential contradiction there because scientists certainly are creative but they are also investigating a reality. They have to prove their theories. It matters a lot for scientists whether their theory is true or false. And that is different from fiction. I thought of that particularly in relation to *The Biographer's Tale*, because in the bit that you were reading Phineas is in his seminar and he is listening to somebody wittering on about "morcellement", a kind of boring Arcadian metaphor. He has heard it a million times. And then in the narrative of Galton, there is that terrible bit where Galton gets to the lake and it is full precisely of dismembered bodies, and it's the real thing, but it's not the real thing, of course, because it's all lies, it's all fiction. So I am not quite sure where that leaves science in the novel, except that Phineas becomes an ecologist.

ASB: That's a different kind of science again. It is quite interesting you've used one of the words against which I have a complete block and I never, ever use, which is "creative". I just can't use it because I think it belongs in religion and I am not a religious person. I would say artistic, I would say constructive, I will say aesthetic, I will say orderly, and I don't say science is creative. I think I really love it because it isn't. Because it doesn't even say it is, because it says it is looking for the truth in places where the truth might be found. It is in fact an agnostic's sense of what human beings can do as opposed to a fear of what they think they can do which they can't do. I am in the odd position of believing only God can create and having no belief at all in God. I talk about constructing, which I think builders can do, and architects can do, and I can do, and people putting together skeletons can do. I didn't create Galton's vision. I invented it out of several things he did record. His description of what the South Africans did to the two young women whose feet they casually cut off was his own writing, that was him and I just pushed it a bit into being Lacan's, as you observed. I made it more like Lacan than it was, but it began as an absolute natural fact, which he had observed.

IS: What's interesting to me is the complex connection between what you know to be part of the life of the character and what is invented, like Galton's dream. Galton writes about this horrible experience of seeing mutilated people in a completely detached way in his letters home. And then he has the dream, which is quite frightening, about separate bits of bodies floating around and disembodied suffering eyes coming towards him. This invented dream, based in what you know about his real experience, has for an analyst such tremendous psychic reality. This is what would happen if you were emotionally cut off from an actual experience because it's so unbearable: it can't just disappear, so it stays in your unconscious mind, and this has consequences. The invented dream has psychic truth.

ASB: It's a very interesting example of starting in truth, or in records and imagining—that is the word I actually used. He did have dreadful nightmares when he got back from Africa. He was a very mild man, Galton, and he expressed surprise that he had such dreadful nightmares because he had thought he was coping with the experience of being there quite well. The moment he got on the ship and was leaving the coast he records how terrible he felt. Then he has this very Christian nightmare about a figure of a crucified person, which he describes as a sort of Roman centurion hanging on the wall of his bedroom, and he says he could see it perfectly clearly, but he knew it wasn't there. So I knew he was a man who could have had this nightmare. Piecing it together from things that I really knew, I just invented the nightmare. I mean, I stuck a bit of Conrad and things in it as well, and it represented the morcellement of Lacan, whom I am not mocking.

Audience: Have you ever written a novel that was sparked by some psychological or philosophical truth that you wanted to tackle?

ASB: Have I ever developed a novel that was sparked off by some psychological or philosophical truth that I want to pass on? I had an email from a fellow writer the other day. I was telling him he should get on with his novel, and he said: "You have things you want to say to the world, and I just like messing around and occasionally writing." And I was terribly hurt by this because I had never seen myself as a person that has anything to say. I want to construct things. I had never really thought that I knew a truth. I think I write novels because I think the truth is a very, very complicated thing and only the constructed object of a novel can give you an inkling of how complicated. I would like to say at this point how interesting it is talking to Ignês, because she knows the way in which to describe psychological truths from a professional theoretical point of view, and she avoids the language, in our conversations, of any kind of theory, don't you, she talks to me like me about objects and things, and facts.

IS: In our conversations you were getting irritated and saying: "Do I have to be the psychoanalyst?" because you thought I was avoiding it.

ASB: Well, I always have a feeling that Ignês knows something that might be called an idea or a truth, and that she is very carefully concealing it from me. And when she does this for long enough I feel that she is observing me, and she really knows what I am talking about and I don't. This is in fact part of the comedy of our continual dialogue. I've never said that before, have I?

IS: No, and it's very naughty of you too. And also it's not really true!

JS: Well, I hate to bring this dialogue to an end but unfortunately ... I would like to say thank you both very, very much for an extremely stimulating and enjoyable hour and half. It has been a pleasure.

Brenda Maddox
in conversation with
Helen Taylor Robinson

Chair: Ruth Robinson
17 November 2000

RR: We are delighted to have the biographer Brenda Maddox here with us this evening, in conversation with the psychoanalyst Helen Taylor Robinson. They will be talking about Brenda's work and in particular her latest book *George's Ghosts: A New Life of W.B. Yeats*. Brenda and Helen will talk for 45 minutes, and then there will be 45 minutes worth of discussion with the audience, after which we hope you'll stay for refreshments—and more discussion.

Helen Taylor Robinson is a psychoanalyst in full time private practice with adults and young people. She has a background in English literature and a longstanding interest in the application of psychoanalysis to the arts.

Brenda Maddox has a career in writing and broadcasting. She worked for *The Economist* for twenty years, latterly as Britain Editor, then as Home Affairs Editor. During this period she covered the conflict in Northern Ireland as well as writing on telecommunications and family law. She has written seven books including her three critically acclaimed biographies. The first, *Nora: A Life of Nora Joyce*, was about Nora Barnacle, the wife of James Joyce. It won *The Los Angeles Times* Prize for Biography and was also shortlisted for the Whitbread Prize for Biography. It was used as a basis for the film *Nora*, released in May of this year, which was directed by a female director, Pat Murphy, with Ewan McGregor and Susan Lynch playing the Joyce couple. Her second biography, *A Married Man: A Life of D.H. Lawrence*, was published in 1994 and won the Whitbread Biography Award. Her most recent book about W.B. Yeats, published last year, was reviewed very positively, with Victoria Glendenning in *The Spectator* describing it as "crisp, humane, sophisticated and sufficient. It tells you everything that anyone except a fanatic would want to know." It was shortlisted this year for the Samuel Johnson non-fiction prize.

Brenda Maddox writes regularly for such publications as *The Observer*, *The New Statesman*, and *The New York Times*. She has been guest presenter on Radio 4's *Start the Week* with Melvyn Bragg and is now a regular contributor to Laurie Taylor's *Room for Improvement* and to arts review programmes on radio. Brenda is American born, now British, and she is of Irish and Italian descent. She lives in London and Wales with her husband, John Maddox, who has had a distinguished career in science journalism. She is currently working on a biography of Rosalind Franklin, the woman scientist who (to quote Brenda) "might have discovered the double helix of DNA if Watson and Crick had not got there first." So now I'd like to invite Helen and Brenda to start their conversation.

HTR: Thank you for inviting both of us to engage in a conversation, which is a difficult thing for a psychoanalyst and an author to do in a straightforward way. I'm offering to begin with my own anxiety about how to interest you, as an audience who may have a great deal of insight, and also have questions and thoughts of your own, which I won't be considering. And there are Brenda's own things that she wants to offer that we may not get to, or have time for.

I'm really grateful to have been asked to start the process, and to be in this, our new building, the home of The British Psychoanalytical Society, for the first time in an official capacity. We are in a moment of change in psychoanalysis, and it's very nice to gather people in from the outside to join us. Ruth has pointed out to me that the *Irish Post* had a small statement in it saying: "Brenda Maddox is going to be 'under the influence of the psychoanalysts' tonight." It struck me that that was an interesting phrase and something that we might well have to think about. There are lots of meanings to that phrase "under the influence".

Whatever I say here tonight doesn't represent psychoanalysis as a whole. It is one individual's expression of a process that is unique to each one of us as psychoanalysts, and yet has a universality about it. I see that as vital to the life of psychoanalysis, that all of us speak very much from our own understanding of what the unconscious in us has produced, and what we have struggled with in relation to it. So whatever I say isn't what psychoanalysis *is*. But I do hope that you will also challenge some of the things that we find ourselves saying.

Something that struck me, Brenda, as I was thinking about the connections between our two professional worlds and the many differences—I feel very conscious that we must sustain that knowledge—was that you could say that psychoanalysis is, in a sense, the biography of Freud. Everything that has subsequently grown, through other figures that have elaborated psychoanalysis into this strange profession, is about biography, in the sense that the only thing that we have to go on, to start with, is our own insights. Of course it's a very specific kind of biography, it's an attempt to address the unconscious self, but it struck me that the whole of psychoanalysis has germinated really from that one man starting to look at the inside of himself. So you could say the whole of psychoanalysis is biography; and all of us add our own biography and shape it in our own way. In starting with the notion that you're a biographer, a literary biographer to begin with, unlike us analysts, you don't have the problem that we have, which is trying to direct our minds to the unconscious side of the self. You have a more open question when you start looking at something.

BM: I told Helen and Ruth when they came to see me a month ago that I don't take a very theoretical approach to what I do, so it's very hard for me sometimes to answer these conceptual things. However, since our earlier conversation I have turned my mind to the thoughts of biography and psychoanalysis and I'd like to say what my first superficial—which are one's deepest—thoughts are.

The one thing that I certainly do share with analysts is a belief that "the child is father to the man". When I write a biography I think the early life counts. I give it a lot of attention and I also believe—I've written biographies recently about writers—that, whoever we are, our words, whether they're written or spoken, reveal more than we initially intend. So I've always got an eye out for what the words are also saying at the same time. In that sense we're in the same street. However, I'm not trying to heal anybody and I'm not in a profession. I do biography as I do journalism, which I've had a long career of and which, when I started, was certainly an honourable profession, and I still think it is. Anybody can do it. If you can get somebody to print your words, you are a writer or a journalist. It's not a profession. A profession, I think, can be described as having entry standards. You have to get approved by a board, and they can kick you out if you don't meet those standards. That is a profession, and you have a licence of some form. That is not true for what I do. So I think that is a big difference.

So I don't have any sense of standards to live up to, except my own, and there's a law of libel. I also have an obligation. People always say to me, and I'm sure they never say it to you, that it must be a "labour of love", whenever I'm doing something. Well, not exactly. I do it for money. I have a good idea, and I talk it around with my agents, and people want to bid on it, and they want to read the book too, so I agree to deliver a book. This is the reality constraint. And there's a timetable, a deadline. I mean this is the wonderful thing about journalism which is probably not true of psychoanalysis: there is an absolute deadline that you have to get it done by, or else. So I'm used to meeting deadlines and one does it, and in the end you have to have a book which is, above all, a package of paper. It's got to be handle-able, although I just reviewed a biography of Wordsworth, and I could not actually hold it in my hand. And if you fall asleep reading a book that heavy, you do serious damage to yourself!

So there's some incentive to make it a manageable passage, and you are always writing, like all journalists do and, I suppose, all biographers do, for two completely different audiences. One audience is the people who know much more about it than I ever will; and the other is the people to whom I am trying to make something clear enough in their terms, and also tell them why I think they should be interested.

So that's what I do. In many ways, I believe, there isn't any such thing as biography. To me it's "a book about". There are so many different ways you can approach a life—political, psychological, royal or whatever. There are many, many ways. It's very handy for booksellers to have one whole section of Waterstone's and you know what you find there. But these books have as much in common with mysteries or thrillers. To behave as if there was a genre, with the rules of the game, isn't the way it is. You just get a book about somebody, or perhaps a whole period in time, but looked at through the focus of a life.

I'll say one last thing, and I think there is a linking point here with psychoanalysis, which is about your relationship to the subject of the biography. The most frequently asked question: people get a funny look in their eye and then they say: "But do you like him?" There's somehow this thought that you have to be half in love with your subject in order to invest so much time. It's just not so. There's got to be something to be said, there's got to be a reason why you're interested, there's got to be a reason why other people might be interested, there's got to be some new material or something new to say because most of them have been done already. All this.

The other question that I'm always asked is: "Do we need another book about that?" Then of course as you go along in your work you come across things that you don't like. I thought that if D.H. Lawrence had had a chance to see the manuscript of my book, it would never have been published. And I thought: "Oh dear, do I really want to go on with it?" You see your subject in the round. And then maybe at the end, like doctors with their patients, you can't help but like them because you've seen them through so much, and you know the other sides of them that perhaps other people haven't seen before. So in that sense I think you don't need to start liking them. I don't know about the biographer of Hitler or a few hard cases, but ordinarily I would think that we probably end up liking our subjects a bit better than we did in the middle of the project.

The other thing that I think maybe we have in common with psychoanalysts is that we have to construct a narrative. Somehow you get all this chaos of experience, of words, whatever, and you have to try and make a pattern to it. And, of course, in biography it helps that life begins and ends. You have to decide where are the climaxes, where are the decision points, where you break off, where you start a new chapter, without being phoney about it, without putting artificial suspense like "But little did he know what terrors were held in store . . ." It's very hard not to be ham-fisted about it and I spend a lot of time worrying about that.

HTR: Here's a strange, rather mad thought that's just occurred to me as I was listening. I was just looking at the size of the biography that Brenda writes, and thinking about narrative, and thinking about similarities and differences between biography and psychoanalysis. I did have this mad thought that if a writer had to include in her text all the pauses, and the silences, and the lack of movement forward in the narrative, all the days when you don't write, all the time when you're not engaged with the work, if you had all the pages that signified when the work is not in progress, what would the biography become, in scale and size? I'm thinking of the parallel with analysts who take as much from the silence, and the gaps, and the language that is *not* a conscious movement forward, and trying to think about this perfectly shaped object, the book. It would be interesting to think what you could put together as a book, that contained the silences, and the absence of meaning, or the absence of language, all those things—we never call that a book. We call a book the words that you *have* selected, which becomes the final picture. I find myself pondering that issue.

BM: Certainly, in writing a life you try to indicate there are years in which nothing much happened, or your subject was depressed, or things didn't go forward. A very hard thing is when a life reaches some high point, which is why people are probably reading the book, but then there's the sloping off, the old age, the illness. You have to get all that in but without giving it commensurate time.

HTR: I was meaning you, as you write and as you pause in your thinking.

BM: That's all the time.

HTR: That's all the time, and you were telling me about your method of work which was . . .

BM: Are you going to tell everybody?

HTR: Yes. I thought it was linked to the way we work, in some ways. You were telling me that you didn't move straight-forwardly through your text. You found a great liberation, you said, in being allowed to go away from what you were writing and tell yourself: "I don't have to finish this now." It's something I tell every student of mine, not to try and straightforwardly answer the question they are posed, but to try to think about not answering it, or to ask: why is this question difficult to answer? I'm thinking about all that kind of interruption in the process of conscious mind that we as analysts take seriously, which is the unconscious and its communications. I'm wondering whether you give yourself any room for "I can't do this now, I really can't do it and I want to drop it, and why can't I do it?"—that kind of interruption.

BM: No, it's not that dramatic. I'm disciplined but not organ-ised, if you can accept those two things as different. I work every day but I don't chain myself to the work-bench. I work at home, which means I'm always going downstairs and signing for a parcel, or marinating something for dinner, or whatever. I wel-come distraction and I've got a very untidy mind, so I shift from the back of the book to the front of the book, and I've learnt to tolerate the fact that I don't do one chapter, finish it, all nice and tidy, and then allow myself to move on. I work on the whole book all at once. I wouldn't advise this for anybody else, it's just the way I do it and it seems reasonable. But what I *do* do is deliver the book. I think there's only two kinds of books, finished and unfinished. I try very hard to finish mine, otherwise you have to give the money back, you see. So I find money is a great incentive, and the fact that somebody out there wants it, has put some money down, and in that sense it's a validation of the project. It gets me through so I don't think that I'm—it's not despair—but I don't demand for myself an orderliness in work which I know other people have. I see them, I admire them, but I don't have it, and the books seem to get done anyway, so I roll with it.

HTR: I suppose I was saying that I do encourage people to do what you're saying don't do. I suppose I'm saying: "Be disorderly!"

BM: I would just say: "Have a reality base." If you've got a contract or a deadline or some reason to teach or something to make sure that you get it out of yourself, then don't forget that. Otherwise you could just wallow around forever.

HTR: Yes, I'd go with that. I was wondering now if the audience would like to hear a passage from the biographies that Brenda has written, to try and focus on what effect they have, or perhaps what someone else, an author, might take out of the material that she's produced. I'm really thinking about difference here. Perhaps I haven't indicated how much I think the psychoanalyst's attention to words is different from that of a writer. There's no constraint on a writer in terms of "What words will I not use or how will I put something?" I'm thinking about the analyst's notion of a structure, a theory of mind, a way of understanding things that might programme language into a much narrower base of meanings than language is capable of. In other words, I am saying that writers continually elaborate usage of language, words and meanings which we, in the consulting room, might not even dream of. I am referring to the possibilities that we have to exclude, as analysts, because we're doing something else, a given task, and we can't bring in all that range. But writers are immensely refreshing because they do. So I think there are huge differences in our understanding and use of words, and huge differences, perhaps, in our notions of what lies *behind* the words.

I wondered about reading a passage to allow the audience into what you've written, as it is difficult to talk about the whole of your work, and I feel we cannot do justice to all the issues that are to do with being a biographer. I thought if we focused on something, we could draw attention to things about it in the second half discussion, and perhaps we two could draw attention to things ourselves now as we look at them. We've decided between us to select a passage from the Yeats book and a passage from the Lawrence book.

You make the point, don't you Brenda, that Yeats, although Irish, was quite English too, quite split in his Irishness. There will be many here who will want to talk about the book on Joyce too, and I haven't got an understanding of Joyce sufficient to be able to talk about him, except for early Joyce, so I'm again restricting us. But I wondered—shall we start with Yeats? There's a chapter here, something small just to link us again, as analysts, with biography. In the *British Journal of Psychotherapy* it so happened that I found an acknowledgement to Brenda in a paper by Paul Schimmel. He's written a paper called "It Is Myself That I Remake—W.B. Yeats's self-construction in life and poetry". At the end of his paper he acknowledges you. He says:

I have just read, after writing this, Brenda Maddox's book, and she also identified the tendency of biographers to overlook the importance of the mother and give detailed consideration to the biographical evidence as to Susan Yeats's, the mother of W.B. Yeats, influence upon her son's life. It is of note that her analysis leads to similar formulations to those put forward in this paper.

So it's a nice link between her biography and this piece of psychoanalytic thinking about an artist. It might allow us to look at a passage about Susan Yeats that you wrote. And you told me that you got criticised for "general" statements, psychoanalytic-type statements, which is very difficult for people not to do these days. You wanted to read a bit and I wanted to comment on one particular line and perhaps we might discuss that afterwards.

BM: All right. My book starts actually not at the beginning of his life but with him getting married at the age of 52, after a lifetime of running away from it all or chasing impossible women. Then the marriage wasn't going well. He'd married a woman he'd met at psychic research meetings, and the marriage wasn't going well at all. Then suddenly, on their honeymoon, she developed this talent for magic writing. She began scrawling words across the page and communicating, bringing him messages from spirits, and this saved the marriage. Then they went on for four or five years doing this communication—which has all now been deciphered by very careful scholars. So it's a kind of crazy side, a silly side of Yeats from which he got metaphors for poetry, and the world is richer for them.

I thought that, having presented him that way, then I would flash back to his childhood and suggest perhaps why he has to go in for this kind of convolution, and why he was actually so late getting round to what most people do a bit earlier, marrying and starting a family. This is my particular prejudice: I hate to pick up a biography about somebody and you start way back with the great great grandfather, who inevitably has the same name (it's James Joyce, but it's not *that* James Joyce, it's the great great grandfather), and the origins of the family money, and the mill, and all this kind of thing. And I've lost interest by the time we come across our boy. So I started with Yeats in full flight in his life, but then I allowed myself, in Chapter 10, and this is considered very eccentric—not that there are any rules in biography, you understand—to tell where the family came from. 1865 was when Yeats was born, and I took some risk in saying this next thing, but I believe it, so what's the point of writing a book if you can't say what you mean?

The secret of Yeats is that his mother did not love him, at least not in any way that warmed him in recollection, or that a child needs for confidence in life. "Whatever else is uncertain in this stinking dunghill of a world," says Cranly in *A Portrait of the Artist as a Young Man*, "a mother's love is not." Susan Yeats's was.

Unlike James Joyce, who drew his supreme cockiness from his mother's faith in him, Yeats grew up without this endorsement. Unlike Joyce, being the eldest by no means made him the favourite. With Lily born fourteen months after his own birth in 1865, and with four more babies arriving by the time he was nine, Yeats was edged to the periphery of the attention of a cold, despondent, over-burdened young woman. Maud Gonne's should not be the first name to spring to mind when reading Yeats's lines about

The folly that man does
Or must suffer, if he woos
A proud woman not kindred of his soul.
                    (*A Dialogue of Self and Soul*)

Susan Pollexfen Yeats was born in Sligo in 1841, died in Bedford Park, London in 1900, was silent, undemonstrative, expressionless. Yet she was at least as great a force in shaping the imagination of her impressionable son as his well-publicised and self-publicising father, and probably greater. When George Yeats (Yeats's wife) told Richard Ellmann that "the mother's influence has been underestimated", she was referring to Susan Yeats's store of Irish folk tales, her narrative gift and her keen sense of the supernatural. That there was a darker side to the maternal legacy was acknowledged when George told Ellmann that Mrs Yeats was a timid and frightened woman and that Yeats suffered from a strong need to justify himself.

His celebrated poem *Among School Children* is powerful evidence. Yeats was already, by then, an Irish Free State senator and a Nobel Laureate. He wrote about himself as "a smiling public man", and he seemed to feel "his mother would not think he'd amounted to much":

What youthful mother, a shape upon her lap . . .
Would think her son did she but see that shape
With sixty or more winters on its head,
A compensation for the pang of his birth,
And the uncertainty of his stepping forth?

Now I'll jump to another book, *Reveries over Childhood and Youth*, the first book of his collection of autobiographies. In this Susan Yeats's presence can be felt from her absence, from a lack of any sense of the comfort she gave. Instead Yeats wrote the chilling line "I remember little of childhood but its pain." He confessed also as a boy that he prayed he would die, even though "there was no reason for my unhappiness". The first faint sketch of his mother that does appear shows her not in any conventional pose of feeding, soothing or scolding, but rather in the act of narration. This is Yeats:

When I think of her, I always see her talking over a cup of tea in the kitchen with our servant, the fisherman's wife, on the only themes outside our house that seemed of interest— the fishing people of Howth, of the pirates and fishing people of Rosses Point. She read no books, but she and the fisherman's wife would tell each other stories that Homer might have told, pleased of any moment of sudden intensity and laughing together over any point of satire.

Now in another passage he says:

She would spend hours listening to stories or telling stories of her own Sligo girlhood and it was always assumed between her and us that Sligo was always more beautiful than other places. I can see now that she had great depth of feeling.

If "Sligo" can be translated as "Mother", Yeats's longing for it becomes a hunger for something more tactile than rural tranquillity, as in this reminiscence from the same *Autobiographies*:

I remember when I was nine or ten years old walking along Kensington High Street, so full of love for the fields and roads of Sligo that I longed—a strange sentiment for a child—for earth from a road there that I might kiss it.

And one more infantile image of a return to the womb or the breast, from his *Memoirs*:

I was going along the Strand and, passing a shop window where there was a little ball kept dancing by a jet of water, I remembered the waters about Sligo and was moved to a sudden emotion that shaped itself into The Lake Isle of Innisfree.

HTR: Although it might be hard to take all that in, there was something in the passage that started me thinking. You are making the point that this man's mother, Susan Yeats, was an enigmatic figure, and a complicated figure for the son to come to terms with, in all sorts of ways. But on the other hand you're saying she was a great influence on his artistic imagination. The line that struck me was Yeats's line "I can see now that she had great depth of feeling". I think sometimes we, as analysts, make the assumption that we do know, and can grasp what a patient is feeling. I wonder about an artist's capacity to sense a depth of feeling, a level of feeling that couldn't get into ordinary life for this mother. It is a picture of the mother as someone very restrained, and yet this woman's feeling being so powerful, coming out in these stories, coming out in these other ways that she expresses herself. I wondered about the son being affected by this. But for the writer it becomes a transformation, doesn't it? It becomes a symbol, it becomes "I *can* say this thing".

This is in contrast with the patient who *cannot transform*, cannot express the feeling without the analyst's help. The feeling is in the room somewhere, and you are possessed by the feeling, and the experience between the analyst and the patient is overwhelming. But the feeling can't be got into words, or the feeling has to be represented, enacted. This is a real sort of counter-position to psychoanalysis, which says you need to try and get things into words. But the idea is here, in Art, that the artist makes some link to the power and the range and the depth of the feeling that is inexpressible in some way. "How can I put this into words?" or "How can I determine this?" And so he goes to something completely different, something visionary, something symbolic, and finds the means to do it. The things that would hold the writer up on the way, which is what requires the analysis ("that this means this, and that means that, and this is why you're feeling like this"—the how and the why that we spend so much of our time doing) this isn't necessary really for the artist at all. It's that bit that he goes away with—and won't let anybody say "it means this, it means that, it means the other"—and transforms. I just found that line so telling about "she had great depth of feeling", and this man knowing something, without anybody having to instruct him in it, and also knowing how to use it in his art. That's the bit that I linked to her effect on him.

BM: That's very interesting. Yeats wouldn't have gone near psychoanalysis because he actually realised this was the source of his imagination, and he was a very successful poet very early on. He realised the power of these images and that the more he could remember the better. He used himself, his own fantasies, as his own raw material. He wasn't going to let anybody analyse them away. In that sense he knew his wealth and he sometimes exacerbated it. If you see the film of *Nora*, he (Joyce) actually used himself, trying to get his wife to act out and have affairs with other people so that he could write about it. Yeats analysed over and over his feelings for his mother and he saw the words that came out. His biggest fear was that the images would dry up and he would not have the source of poetry. And of course that's what he got from his supposed "ghost"—George's dictated writings.

HTR: I suppose we would say that coming in too soon, and the use of the more conscious mind, would mean the drying up of the images. The coming in too quickly of "I think it means this". Something that doesn't allow it to linger in the most painful way. Not all feelings are painful. It may sound very romantic, but it's something I feel quite deeply about: what may not come into analysis, and it is that what informs our capacity actually to be alive with our patients is not what we've understood about ourselves but what we are still very much struggling with in ourselves, but not particularly consciously. Anyway, it was the beauty of an unspoken connection with his mother that he spent the rest of his life possibly re-working in some way that I liked in that passage.

There's another absolutely beautiful piece of D.H. Lawrence that you quote that I wanted to talk about, but we are getting short of time. Have we run out of time?

RR: Five minutes.

HTR: We've got five minutes. We might come back to it in the second half. I don't know whether we're going right away from what the audience are interested in and I'm concerned about linking up to them and what they're feeling.

BM: If we take some questions, and then, if we want to, we can go back.

HTR: You may not want to come in on this now, you may want to come in on something else, but if we had time for the bit of Lawrence from Brenda's book, it would be nice later. It's terribly easy to be misunderstood, but I'm trying to get across something about a sort of picture you've got there, held together, a picture that spoke something to me at that moment about levels of feelings that we are all possessed by, that we are subject to, whether they be in fantasy or whatever. They really inform our minds in ways that we can really give very little account of, I suppose, and we're grateful to artists when they touch the feeling in some way, move so close to it.

BM: I'll just say a bit about Lawrence. Again, as a writer, you can't write dodging the critics but certainly the word "psycho-babble" isn't one that you hope to see in a review. On the other hand, if you are conscious of the unconscious in these early relationships, you try sometimes to get it in without it showing too much. One of the passages you selected I think does show a lot about Lawrence but I certainly didn't hide my theory. In any case, as you probably know, D.H. Lawrence ran away with his professor's wife, Frieda. They ran off to Germany and she left behind three children, and he was very unsympathetic to her grieving for the loss of these children. So I say in this Lawrence book:

> Lawrence is widely thought to have been impervious to Frieda's anguish over the loss of her children. Hard-heartedness is consistent with his infantile streak. Having lost his mother, he stole another, and demanded she be nobody's mother but his.
>
> Yet just as he harboured dreams of fatherhood, there was hidden inside himself a secret stepfather, a kindly man who knew exactly what Frieda's children were going through and how he would comfort them. In all literature there may be no finer picture of a stepfather and stepdaughter than that of Tom Brangwen and Anna in *The Rainbow*. In a famous passage it is the stepfather who knows how to solace a child screaming (as the Weekley children had never been allowed to do): "I want my mother!" And Lawrence shows, in a brilliant touch, as Tom feeds the cows with one arm, holding Anna in the other, how parents willingly handicapped themselves for the love of a child.
>
> Tom has married Anna's mother, Lydia, a Polish widow. She becomes pregnant, and when she goes into labour, little Anna is not allowed to see her. All this has been explained to her but she repeats: "I want my mother, I want my mother—" and a bitter, pathetic sobbing that soon had the soft-hearted Tilly [the maid] sobbing too. The child's anguish was that her mother was gone, gone.

Tom, as stepfather, tries to intervene. The girl will not listen. She refuses to go to bed; she will not have a drink; she will not stop sobbing. Tom is at first angry, then indifferent, then inspired. "Nay," he says, "it's not as bad as that." He wraps Anna in his mother's shawl and takes her out to the barn while he feeds the cows.

> He opened the doors upper and lower and they entered into the high, dry barn that smelt warm even if it were not warm. He hung the lantern on the nail and shut the door. They were in another world now. The light shed softly on the timbered barn, on the whitewashed walls and the great heap of hay; instruments cast their shadows largely, a ladder rose to the dark arch of a loft. Outside there was the driving rain, inside the softly-illuminated stillness and calmness of the barn. Holding the child on one arm he set about preparing the food for the cows, filling a pan with chopped hay and brewer's grains and a little meal. The child, all wonder, watched what he did. A new being was created in her for the new conditions. Sometimes, a little spasm, eddying from the bygone storm of sobbing, shook her small body. Her eyes were wide and wondering, pathetic. She was silent and quite still.

Anna puts her arm around his neck.

> . . . and the two sat still listening to the snuffing and breathing of cows feeding in the sheds, communicating with this small barn. The lantern shed a soft, steady light from one wall. All outside was still in the rain. He looked down at the silky folds of the paisley shawl. It reminded him of his mother. She used to go to church in it. He was back again in the old irresponsibility and insecurity, a boy at home.

So then I say:

> Tom has taken Anna out of herself and brought her into
> contact with a world beyond her mother, shown her other
> forms of love and life. The passage shows Lawrence at his
> best. With vivid particularity and intense sympathy he creates
> a scene which, powerfully and unobtrusively, preaches a
> message that transcends anything he wrote about sex. In the
> rain, in the darkness, Tom Brangwen humbly senses that
> beyond human beings, beyond even the plant and animal
> kingdom, "There was the infinite world, eternal, unchanging,
> as well as the world of life."

HTR: There's a picture here, as you described it, of the
stepfather's capacity to relate to this little child. I mean the fact
is, as Lawrence says right at the end, it is the external reality, isn't
it, that has completely drawn Tom and the child in, like a great
umbrella over them. The two of them are huddled inside the
reality of the farm, the cows, the rain, the evening. It's absolutely
beautiful. It creates a universe, in a human way, and the child
becomes full of wonder and reduces her sobbing. It was just that
you saw it, didn't you, very much as a capacity for the stepfather
to be able to offer the stepchild something.

I was discussing it with my husband. It was that line about
the mother's shawl. It is the psychoanalyst chipping in here.
When Tom takes her out wrapped in the shawl of his mother,
he is able to identify with being a child, and remember being a
child, in relation to a parent. Maybe that's what makes a good
stepfather. But it's not so much "I can be a good father to you",
it's more that he's suddenly completely overwhelmed by being
a child again. The wrapping in the shawl, the memory of mother,
and going to church all come back. I'm looking at something
that feels like a powerful statement on behalf of our work, which
is what you said, that we do privilege the child, the instinctual

self, and that Lawrence does catch that kind of instinctual self in that moment. At that moment he can become small and they can both feel small inside this—well you could call it a mother, I suppose—this universe, or perhaps inside this experience, rather than trying to dominate the experience, or manage it in some sort of way. They both have to give up, don't they, and their humanity grows as a result of it. It felt like that to me.

BM: Let me just say that that was Lawrence in fiction. He never touched his stepchildren, he never saw them again, he never let their mother see them openly. She had to creep along the road and see them secretly when she was in London. So this was the absolute. He knew what he should have been, and his memories of his own mother were very warm, but he also knew when he wrote that passage, that he had created the condition in which those children were sobbing for their mother, and he had actually taken her away and was not giving her back. He was always very, very clear that he came first.

HTR: Which is another way of perhaps thinking about whether artists really do reach what we psychoanalysts call the Depressive Position (postulated by Melanie Klein), or whether there is absolutely no way in which they do. Rather, that at the moment they are creating something, they do not feel concerned. They feel concerned for something *greater* than the ordinary day to day concerns that we get caught up with, expressed in their concern for *their symbolic reality,* and being concerned for, and true to that. Thank you.

BM: Thank you.

RR: We shall now open it to the audience for comments, questions.

Audience: I had the privilege of having taken part in the conversation about this particular passage. It made me think of
something that you were both saying earlier in relation to similarities and differences. I'm a psychiatrist who always sits on a
fence, so I feel I'm in between two positions: that is, the difference between the biography that we all think of as important, as
clinicians, and the history that we have from a patient which,
in the analytic setting, may not even be taken right at the beginning, but is something that's gleaned throughout the process of
psychoanalysis, whereas a psychiatrist might spend the hour
getting the history.

The obvious difference, from the biographer's point of view,
is that usually the history is gathered from other evidence,
evidence from other people who knew the person, documents
and so on. This is the way in which we formulate, in our own
minds, a biography of somebody, with those different sorts of
evidence. As a psychiatrist I teach my students that they can't
always trust what the patient tells them, sadly, and they have to
actually get external evidence to back it up.

But where does the true interest lie? Is it really important to
know what actually happened in reality? Is it really important
to know whether Lawrence did, or didn't, do something to
Frieda in relation to her children, or do we read from his books
and infer something from that? The psychoanalyst might well
have had a very different picture of Lawrence, from what he
divulged on the couch, from what Brenda's been able to glean
about his history and his life from external evidence. It was just
those sorts of differences that occurred to me—those questions,
where do we start, and where do we stop, and when are we
satisfied, and when are we not?

HTR: That's the whole question, isn't it, of truth and fiction and
illusion and what counts as a meaning. A different discipline will
take a different view on what counts as *the* meaning. What is the

thing I'm going to privilege? That's terribly important in terms of difference, and we have every right, don't we, to distinguish in that way.

BM: Well, as I said before, you're trying to heal somebody.

HTR: Well, what is it *we* do? Some people in the audience might feel they want to say what they think we do. Does anybody else want to say what we do? I was going to say what Freud said, or what Freud was supposed to have said, which is even more difficult. What Freud was reputed to have said, according to a writer who was analysed by Freud and who was claiming this is what he said in her analysis (so how do we know what he said?)—he said that analysis was not a cure-all, that it was a very, very difficult philosophy, and that he felt most people didn't understand what he was trying to put forward, and that our attempts to say "yes, we do understand" are often *mis*understandings.

Audience: I have a question for Mrs Maddox. Have you ever been tempted to heal a reputation?

BM: I'm not a healer. Nobody else is either, it turns out! (*laughing*)

BM: Actually I'm writing about somebody now who *was* much maligned, Rosalind Franklin, the scientist. She came out rather badly in Watson's book, *The Double Helix*. I suppose I believe in the facts. This sounds terribly pretentious, but I'm just trying to find out as much as I can about how things really are, or were, and if that heals a reputation . . . But I certainly wouldn't suppress evidence that actually showed that the critics were right. If you put somebody in the context of their life, and their mother, and various other things, that *does* heal a reputation, I suppose, but that isn't my motive. All the books I've written, I've written for a reason, and mainly because there was some new material. I thought, if I don't go through this and add it to the record, nobody else will. Here is new material that says something I feel deserves calling to people's attention, and that is my motivation. Healing doesn't really come into it.

Audience: I've come with a quite detailed question for Brenda Maddox about something that she says in the Yeats book which bears very much on Helen's point a few minutes ago, that of whether the artist can hold a position in the act of creation and actually also provide the healing properties of art. When you were talking about Yeats I was thinking of how in the 1930s, when he becomes so right-wing, he writes all these loathsome things about eugenics. I quite agree with you that they are loathsome, but I think he does something with them, in the poetry, which utterly transforms them. I'm thinking in particular of your interpretation of *The Statues*, where I think you said—I'm sorry, I left behind my copy of your book, but I think I remember it right—you pick up, which many critics haven't, the essential masturbatory element of the kids "pale from the imagined love / of solitary beds" pressing "at midnight in some public place / live lips upon a plummet-measured face". He was meaning they're full of masturbatory lust.

BM: Well, masturbation will never get a better phrase than that.

Audience: *(continuing)*   No, exactly! If we carry on, I think you said at the end of that passage that Yeats compares the great men of the Irish Rebellion with the great men of the Classical world. I think it's more complicated than that, you see.

BM: Can it be?

Audience: *(continuing)*   Hold on. Because you get this beginning: statues are given meaning by the masturbatory factor, say. Then he makes this extraordinary claim that it was the artists, not the Athenian navy that defeated the Persian invasion of Greece. Then you get this wonderful bit where he takes that vast, fat statue of Victoria as Empress of India and makes it into a sort of mad Buddha feeding on its own death. No clear meaning at all. Then finally, when he writes:

> When Pearse summoned Cuchulain to his side
> What stalked through the Post Office? What intellect
> What calculation, number, measurement replied?
> We Irish, born into that ancient sect
> But thrown upon this filthy modern tide
> And by its formless spawning fury wrecked,
> Climb to our proper dark, that we may trace
> The lineaments of a plummet-measured face.

Now I think that there are two positions there. One is, yes, the Irish rebels were like Caesar setting out to conquer the world—like Michelangelo painting the Sistine Chapel roof (see *Long-legged Fly* in *Last Poems*); but they're also the masturbating adolescents. Now if you bear with me, just to set a bit of background to Yeats: an early reference in *Easter 1916*, "Too long a sacrifice / Can make a stone of the heart", and then later on, in *The Circus Animals' Desertion*,

> I thought my dear must her own soul destroy
> So did fanaticism and hate enslave it,
> And this brought forth a dream and soon enough
> The dream itself had all my thought and love.

—that's a sort of paranoid "statue making". But then you get a quite different tradition. For instance in *Byzantium*: "those images that yet fresh images beget", or *Among School Children*:

> Both nuns and mothers worship images,
> But those the candles light are not as those
> That animate a mother's reveries
> But keep a marble or a bronze repose
> And yet they too break hearts.

I want to complement Helen's question. Do we need to include in artistic creation the Paranoid Schizoid Position (again postulated by Melanie Klein), so that it can be thought about before the real healing creative process can get started?

BM: I think that's a question for Helen, but let me compliment you on your reading and memory of these wonderful lines. It is very hard to quote Yeats. I will just say one thing, as a literary biographer. I'm not a literary critic, but at every point you have to decide: are you going to give the literary work of this fantastically complex and great poet all the various permutations and meanings, or are you going to get on with your narrative? So I certainly don't try to give a full interpretation of any poem. Certainly I say what I feel is the minimum that needs to be said, for the readers I'm writing for, who know even less about it than I do, without offending those who know far more than I ever will.

HTR: I was going to say that your book might elicit a response. You can't do all the literary criticism, but it might generate some thinking, as it has here, for this person, by bringing some things together.

BM: I will say I do try very hard. I might only have four lines in which to say what *Sailing to Byzantium* means, and Richard Ellmann wrote whole books on this, but I at least try to get as accurate a précis as possible of why this work was important, what it meant to him, what it meant to the people around him, before I then pass on to the other events in his life. It does slow you down.

But I quite agree with you there, I've discussed that poem, *The Statues*, with people, and I've said that the interesting thing was his actually linking the classic theme with the Irish Revolution in 1916, and that is all I said about it; but certainly that's not all that's to be said about *The Statues*, which is one of my favourite poems.

HTR: I am thinking now about words themselves, in the poetry we have been hearing, words being pretty. We're just so grateful that words are pretty aren't we, because they soothe us in their prettiness. But I was just thinking about having to write about things which are not so pretty, or don't have the pretty verse to soothe us. It was reminding me of Beckett and his theme of the continual wish to tell another story, you know, to use words to keep us from the real hurt and pain of life. "Let's tell another story," let's do something to while away time in *Waiting for Godot* or *Endgame*. Just by the sound of words, can we just get some words outside of us, out there to stop this stuff that's going on inside?

Audience: Going back to the themes of healing and feeling, I'm a psychoanalyst, and quite recently we were discussing the differences between psychoanalysis and psychotherapy. One of the important things coming out of this was that the recommendation to "know thyself" is, more than likely, therapeutic. So psychoanalysis, I hope, couldn't be said *not* to be therapeutic in its outcome. It made me think of how people who are creative—artists, writers, musicians—are often quite frightened of the prospect of entering into analysis, because of this fear that somehow the creative juices, once known and understood, will just dry up. I'm very interested myself in the power of literature to be so profoundly moving, like the writing of D.H. Lawrence, and how some passages just grab you and just make you go pale, or cry, or something very profound hits you. Yet some passages, which are obviously supposed to do just that, singularly fail. I'm not a writer, and I'm sure there must be a craft to it, but I feel there's much more than a craft to it. In both literature and in psychoanalysis, I think that the way in which a powerful feeling can be evoked in both the reader and the psychoanalyst is a fascinating process. It's important and theoretically interesting and useful for analysts to try to understand how it comes about that one is so profoundly moved by something that a patient says, or something that goes on in the room. I'm not sure about whether or not it is important for writers to know about how to get their work to evoke powerful feelings. Or can you have some control over that? Is it worth trying to work that out? I'm sure it's all written about in literary criticism, but is it just a talent which should be left, to sort of bloom untouched?

BM: I don't think art is that unconscious. I think people know their craft. They may be trying to do something very different than other people have tried to do, but they know what they're doing. There's a wonderful anecdote about Joyce, meeting his friend Frank Budgen in Zurich, and he said: "What have you done?" And Joyce said: "I spent the whole day, or was it two days, writing one sentence ... It's not that I lack the words, it's just the order of the words." And the words were "perfume of embraces all him assailed", or something like this, and he spent several days trying to get them in a way that satisfied him. But it's certainly a very conscious process. And Lawrence was a very good teacher. He started out as a schoolteacher in Croydon, and I think he was probably a very, very good schoolteacher; but he wrote advice to friends of his about keeping it vivid, keeping it short, don't use too much style, a little is more than most folks can understand, and more or less *show*, rather than *tell*. You try to bring it alive, and at least the writers I've written about knew very well how to do this. Yeats spent hours trying to get the right effect across in the wonderful poem *The Wild Swans at Coole*:

The trees are in their autumn beauty
The woodland paths are dry.

He wrote it about fifty different times. If you see how that started out, how he moved all those words around and around and around until finally, like Joyce's image, it comes like a chink of a coin on glass: "Ah, that's what I want." So no, I don't think they're too airy-fairy or unconscious about the effect they're trying to produce.

Audience: I'm a lay person as far as analysis is concerned, but I do know that psychoanalysts have certain safety nets to avoid having too much of themselves coming out in the analysis of their patients. What do you do, as you write—I mean I just think of Lawrence and Yeats, two really tortured souls, and if I were talking about them, I'd probably describe them in reference to myself—how do you avoid letting yourself come out too much in the biography, or are there these safety nets like analysts have?

BM: Well, I suppose it's a sense of proportion. Obviously, certain things touch your own experience and you say: "Well, I know what that's like because I went through it." But it would change the shape of the whole thing if you let your own childhood run away with a story. Just to turn it the other way round, I think I know when to plug in, when I've got something that touches some chord in me, and I can release something I've always thought about, and then I don't hold back. I mean when I was a kid in Massachusetts, we had a neighbour next door who used to weep every St Patrick's Day because she wasn't in South Boston, seeing the parties that were going on, and she'd think about what they were doing in Ireland. It's just the memory of how sad I felt for her, and I wondered what the parties were like. When I read about Nora Joyce, wishing she was back home in Galway on Halloween, I just kind of plugged in and used it; but I wouldn't let it, I hope, run away with the whole chapter.

Again, the stepfather thing: I wrote a whole book about step-parents and how tough I found it, but certainly I sympathised. I used that in the Lawrence we read earlier, but I hope there was not too much of me in it. It's keeping in mind what your reader wants. Biography is like an enormous jigsaw: you've got a frame, you know you need certain pieces, you go out and look for them, and you know when it's done. In that sense you keep this proportion of the whole—too much style can spoil the whole picture. So one would hope to keep it in proportion. When Yeats said all those terrible things about "base-born products of base beds", which again I think are about the best phrases eugenics is ever going to have, he was so ambivalent about it, the way he was about everything. He wasn't a wholehearted fascist. He wasn't that committed to anything wholeheartedly except writing, and getting his own poems done the way he wanted. To me that almost made it forgivable. I didn't take any of his political themes, except his very good pursuit of a very handsome coinage for Ireland, which I thought was totally admirable and took time away from his creative activity. I was very, very impressed by him actually being a working senator. I could have recoiled from the horror of his politics, and we know what happened afterwards that tied in with that whole fascist movement, but it just didn't seem worth it; he didn't seem a real fascist to me, but maybe that was just protecting myself because I had to finish the book!

Audience: I think psychoanalysts are terribly interested, and have always been, in the nature of creativity. What is it? Where did it come from, if you like? If someone wants to ask that question of someone who is a literary biographer, because you're working with creativity and your own, obviously . . . I think Freud, where he talks about Michelangelo, says that great art is that which puts one in touch with what it was in the author or the creative artist which moved them to create. I wondered whether that had any bearing on your choice of who you write about. In your literary biography, is the question of creativity something that you consciously engage with?

BM: No, it's not a concept I've ever been comfortable with. I mean I think everybody's creative. I hope my accountant is creative! (*laughing*) It just requires some imagination to bring strange things together. I suppose some professions would encourage this more than others. The Royal Society had a symposium about creativity in the sciences and in the humanities. It brought together all kinds of very, very worthy people to say great things, and they debated the proposition of Coleridge that it takes five hundred Newtons to make one Shakespeare. In other words, it takes *more* creativity to be a writer. Or, as some people have said, if Beethoven hadn't written his 9th Symphony, nobody else would have. If Watson hadn't discovered the double helix, Rosalind Franklin would have, or somebody else would have. So science is about just discovering what is there, but the arts are making something new.

I don't know about whether science is creative, but I don't think of what I do as creative. It's just a sense that you allow your imagination to bring unlike things together, and I'm sure that's what you do in analysis. You just don't demand too many tight rules. I think it's rather insulting to other people to say "I'm a creative person and what you do is just your job." I mean, teaching is creative! You just have to think: what do I do now, how do I get this across? It just so happens I've chosen three writers in a row, but it's been fortuitous as much as anything. I wouldn't have done the Yeats had Macmillans not published three huge volumes of this communication with supposed spirits, annotated by the University of Florida. It's just a goldmine. It talks about analysis, and you read it, and you think: what are these people saying to each other? It was just blush making, a kind of marriage manual and yet all dressed up as something else. Anyway, I just thought: someone needs to look at this, now that they've translated all this mirror writing and put it down where we can read it. I just wanted my say in what was there. And I've always liked Yeats's poetry since I was an under-graduate. It's just something new to say that draws me, but I kind of shudder when people say "creative".

HTR: I was going to respond with a statement of Picasso's, but of course it's a statement of Picasso's that we have attributed to Picasso. Who knows why he was saying it, and what it means. Picasso says: "A painter paints . . ."—I'm just thinking about Freud's notion of why we're creative—"A painter paints to unload himself of feelings and visions. People seize on the painting to cover up their nakedness. They get whatever they can, wherever they can. In the end I don't believe they get anything at all, they simply cut a coat to the measure of their own ignorance." Quite difficult really to think about, but I was struck by that compression of different ideas. Actually it's a beautiful line, isn't it? That everything we shape out of our understanding is out of our own ignorance. It's in the definition of our own ignorance that we grow. If psychoanalysis has given me anything wonderful it has given me that. "I thought it was like this, but it's totally not like this"; and how such change informs your life and transforms your life. That doesn't have to destroy knowledge, does it? It's a sort of counterweight to an experience, and I suppose an artist gives you that counterweight to your own experience. "I thought it was like this, and what's this now?" Defining the world or measuring or shaping or creating, we don't tend to think of it as shaped by ignorance, but that might be what prompts the artist to put the first touch to something. But it is a wonderfully gratifying something. As to psychoanalysis, I think that it allows you both to feel exposed, terribly exposed, and yet simultaneously to feel you've mastered something, you've understood something. It's a complicated dynamic, but I think if you don't keep it at that, if we become the masters of all understanding, then we're terrifying aren't we?

Audience: I wanted to make a point. You used a phrase earlier which I thought was very telling, you said: "Words have more meanings than we dream of." I thought, in psychoanalysis we don't just work with words, we work with dreams, which are images. This made me have a rather trivial association, which is that in biographies there are usually photographs, people are presented through photographs, images, which is another way of presenting the person. I wondered if you had anything to say about that.

BM: Oh yes. So much work goes into finding the photographs, finding who owns the copyrights to the photographs. That takes as much time as writing the text, and trying to get photographs that aren't the same ones that have been in other biographies. I'm sure you're like me as a reader: you look at the photographs first and then you see whether you want to go back and read about whoever it is.

RR: Well, I'm afraid we'll have to stop there now. I'd like to thank Helen and Brenda for a very interesting conversation and I hope people will stay for a glass of wine.

Reference

Schimmel, P. (2000). 'It is myself that I remake': W. B. Yeats's Self Construction in Life and Poetry. *British Journal of Psychotherapy*, 17(1): 71–84.

Philip Pullman
in conversation with
Marie Bridge

Chair: John Churcher
24 January 2003

JC: Good evening to everybody. On behalf of the British
Psychoanalytical Society I would like to welcome the many
friends and guests who are here. My name is John Churcher and
I shall be chairing the discussion this evening.

This evening we welcome as a distinguished guest the writer
Philip Pullman, the author of *Northern Lights*, *The Subtle Knife* and
The Amber Spyglass, the three novels for children and adults which
make up the trilogy *His Dark Materials*.

Formerly a teacher of English, Philip Pullman has published
quite a number of books over the last thirty years, mainly for
children and young people, and more recently his work has
become very widely known, particularly after *The Amber Spyglass*,
published in 2000—and published after a long and anxious wait
by many of his readers—won him the prestigious Whitbread
Prize. All three books of the trilogy have since been produced on
tape and on CD as unabridged talking books, read by Philip with

a supporting cast, and most recently a shorter, dramatised adaptation of them has been broadcast on BBC Radio 4.

In conversation with Philip Pullman this evening will be the psychoanalyst Marie Bridge, who is a member of the British Psychoanalytical Society with a background in the study of literature; she and Philip have met once some weeks ago to begin the conversation. I will shortly invite them to continue this with us.

In planning this event, Marie and I thought that the main topic should be the books themselves and the characters, the themes, the worlds within them and the issues raised by them. The relationship between psychoanalysis and literature is a reciprocal one; it's a two way street, and as psychoanalysts we felt that we had much to learn from what Philip Pullman has created.

Among the audience there will be some of you, I'm sure, who have read all three books already, and some may even have read them for the second or third time; others may be in the middle of reading them still, or perhaps still waiting for a chance to read them when someone else has finished; and yet others perhaps may still be thinking about getting round to reading them one day; so we're a kind of mixed audience.

Now I would like to invite Philip Pullman and Marie Bridge to continue their conversation, and I think Marie is going to speak first.

MB: I'm going to put to one side for this evening my enormous admiration for you as a storyteller and my enormous admiration for the way you write, the way you manage to convey what rage feels like, terror feels like, joy, desire feels like. I want to put all that literary stuff to one side and to think with you about what particularly excites me as a psychoanalyst in your writing, and to look at particular themes, which interest me in my work and that I found really resonating throughout your novels in the trilogy. For people who don't know the stories would it be fair

to say that the trilogy is a reworking, almost a reversal of the
Genesis myth?

PP: Of that part of the Genesis story that happens in Chapter 3,
which is the story of the Temptation and the Fall, as they're
known, the creation of Adam and Eve. In the biblical story
there was a prohibition in place: they mustn't eat the fruit of
the Tree of Knowledge. And then the serpent, who was more
subtle than all the other beasts of the field, came and said: "If
you eat the fruit of that you'll become wise." Eve, according to
the Genesis story, was tempted and ate the fruit and gave it to
her husband and he ate. And the first thing that happened was
that they became aware that they were naked. They hadn't
noticed this before. You'd think they would, wouldn't you, but
it hadn't occurred to them! That's what it's about. Suddenly they
became aware of something that they hadn't been aware of
before, they became self-conscious and so they made themselves
clothes; and when God came along he at once spotted the
difference! "You've got clothes on," he said, "what's going on?"
And so they had to admit that they'd eaten the fruit of knowledge
and had broken, disobeyed his command, and they were thrown
out of the Garden of Eden as a result and had to live in sorrow
and pain and misery, and serves them right, according to the
traditional story.

You mentioned it's a reversal, a moral reversal here. Well
yes, that's what I was sort of doing. This is a fascinating story,
and I've long been absorbed by it and absorbed by a wonderful
commentary on this story by the German romantic Heinrich von
Kleist, who wrote an essay entitled *On the Marionette Theatre* in
about 1810, where he looks at the story of Chapter 3 of the Book
of Genesis in terms of what it means about growing up and
becoming aware of ourselves, and self-conscious, and losing that
childlike grace, and becoming clumsy and self-aware and awkward in one's life. He points out that there's no way back, which

is symbolised in this story by the angel with the flaming sword that stands at guard: you can't get back; once you're out, it's finished. The only way to re-enter Paradise, says Kleist, is go all the way around the world experiencing life and suffering and sorrow and trouble and difficulty, but learning all the while until eventually, if you live long enough, you will re-enter Paradise, as it were, through the back door. This seems to me to be a very good description of the two states of innocence and wisdom; so this is the sort of spectrum of things, the spectrum of life experiences that I'm talking about in the story.

MB: And in the great conflict in your novel between the forces of good and the forces of evil, that which, broadly speaking, signifies the good—the quest for knowledge, to enjoy the world we live in, to try and understand in the greater and greater complexity, to have more tolerance—all that is symbolised by the choice of human sexuality.

PP: Yes.

MB: I find that particularly interesting as it's so close to Freud's original theory of the libido, which began as a theory of sexuality but came, towards the end of his life, to mean something much wider than that, to mean all those things that are on the side of life. Towards the end of Freud's life he began to think that the force which was against all that is on the side of life was something that he came to call the "death instinct". People have conceptualised it in different ways, but one way of looking at it is a kind of deadly inertia, a kind of deadly, anti-life force which undoes all the things that we try to create, and which remains an ongoing struggle in our lives. I felt that in the novels you capture this, you describe this so beautifully in the figures of Spectres.

PP: The Spectres of Indifference, yes.

MB: Precisely; perhaps you can talk about the Spectres?

PP: The Spectres of Indifference are ghost-like figures that the two young protagonists of the story encounter in the second book, where they meet. They meet in a deserted city, deserted by adults, that is to say, as the children are still there living wild and free. Every so often the Spectres come, and the adults have to go away because the Spectres can attack the adults, but the children seem to be invulnerable to the Spectres for some mysterious reason. Now the Spectres for me had quite a long and complicated history. Part of it comes from William Blake, who mentions Spectres in one of his poems. I'm trying to get the exact wording now but it's always terribly difficult. When you're about to quote something it goes, doesn't it?

MB: I've brought my books with me! [i.e. *His Dark Materials*]

PP: I could probably quote myself, but I'm not sure about Blake. He says we must get rid of our Spectres; we must cast away our Spectres. Why are they Spectres of Indifference? Because of my own experiences with depression, when it seems to me that the life and the meaning and the colour drains out of everything and leaves you indifferent, indifferent to your own self as well as anything else. It occurred to me that the opposite of depression is not happiness. There's not just unhappiness and happiness. The opposite of depression is energy. So that's what the Spectres of Indifference do. Why they do it, and where they come from, is a question that's a bit more complicated, so perhaps we'll leave that; but that's the place they have in the story. And children are immune, children can walk among them unharmed; it's the adults who are vulnerable. Again it's a bit complicated to explain why, but it seems to work.

MB: I was going to ask you if you would read one brief passage to give the audience just a flavour of the way you write.

PP: Of course.

MB: Would you like to set it in context yourself?

PP: Yes. This happens towards the end of the second book when a witch . . . and the witches are figures of good in the story. (I keep having to pause and say what I mean by that, and then come back and say what I mean by that, an infinite regression.) You mentioned a little while back the struggle between good and evil; that's what it looks like from the outside because of course we're on one side and we're against the other side, as that's how stories work. In real life it's never that simple, it's always a struggle between "goods". People on the other side think they're good and we're evil, you know, it's like that, and that's a more interesting way of looking at it. However, for the moment witches are on the side of our heroes. A witch has been lured, tempted by the mother of Lyra, the child, a woman called Mrs Coulter, who is a very important figure in the book, powerful, glamorous, sexy, dangerous, unpredictable too. The witch has been lured by Mrs Coulter into danger and the Spectre attacks her . . . I've just spotted something else I have to explain, sorry! In the first sentence here I refer to the witch's daemon. Those who have read the books will know, but for those who haven't I'll just say briefly that in Lyra's world everybody goes through life accompanied by their daemon, and the daemon is an aspect of yourself which is external and visible and has the form of an animal. That's all you need to know for the moment. It's the daemon which the Spectres go for.

And Mrs Coulter drew herself up and snapped her fingers to the Spectre feeding on the witch's daemon. The little snow bunting daemon lay twitching on the rock as the Spectre moved towards the witch herself, and then whatever Lena Feldt [the witch] had undergone before was doubled and trebled and multiplied a hundredfold. She felt a nausea of the soul, a hideous and sickening despair, a melancholy weariness so profound that she was going to die of it. Her last conscious thought was disgust at life: her senses had lied to her; the world was not made of energy and delight but of foulness, betrayal, and lassitude. Living was hateful and death was no better, and from end to end of the universe, this was the first and last and only truth. Thus she stood, bow in hand, indifferent, dead in life.

And that's how I describe the Spectre attacking Lena Feldt, the witch.

MB: It's absolutely beautiful, and so close to what I think Freud was talking about in terms of the death instinct.

PP: I think what I was describing was depression, my experience with it, that's what I had to go on. Was Freud talking about depression when he wrote this?

MB: I think it was one of the things he was talking about, certainly.

PP: The depression is one of the weapons in the arsenal of death, is that right?

MB: Yes, that's a good way of putting it. Can I lead you into something else now, because I want to go back to what you were saying about good and evil and that there is no clear-cut good and evil in the novel.

PP: In the world. The novel is clearer because stories have to be simplified a bit in order to make things clear. Sorry, I interrupted, carry on.

MB: One of the things that really struck me is that a very important theme of your novel is corruption. There's a lot of decay, sewage, smell, all the bad characters or the bad figures, the harpies, the tualapi, and so on, you identify them with a bad smell. One of the things that leapt out at me reading your novel is that filth, which you talk about a lot, is the other side of Dust, and Dust is goodness, Dust is consciousness, yes?

PP: Dust with a capital D.

MB: Yes, Dust with a capital D. Dust is regarded by the Church as sin, but in terms of your thinking Dust is what is good and what we live for.

PP: Yes.

MB: And yet that very same Dust is also, looked at in another way, filth. I wondered if one of the things that you were getting at is that everything that we most value: love, sexuality, knowledge, science, anything could also be used in a perverse way for evil; it's very, very striking as a theme.

PP: Now it's there I see what you mean. I'd like to say I was getting at it, but I didn't know I was. This is the value of psychoanalysts, you see, they tell you things you didn't suspect! Yes, I see that now, it's very interesting, but it hadn't occurred to me, actually. If I was a bit sharper, I would say: "Yes, I thought of that all the way through. I had that in mind. I'm glad you picked it up, well done!"

MB: A good example of this would be the way Mrs Coulter can use her intuitive understanding of Will's attachment to his mother. This is something good, that she as a mother can identify with. But then she can use this identification between herself and Will's mother, what analysts would call the transference, in this terribly perverse way to trap him. I think that's beautifully described.

PP: I'm glad I was being psychoanalytical there. I really didn't have that in mind. It just seemed to me that that's the way this sort of person would act. I suppose when you're describing characters in action, when you're writing a story, you must be basing it on people you've observed, things you've seen, or things you've read about in other fiction, but not always consciously. One of the traps you fall into, and one of the great dangers that we're all aware of, is of writing a scene which is terrific and wonderful, and then you go and read it in somebody else's book, which you then remember you read last year. So a lot of what happens when you're making up a character in action, and showing them in action, comes directly out of your own experience. Some of it comes out of what you've read in other books, some of it you just make up. You extrapolate from what you've seen people doing and you think: "Well, if we just give the scene another little twist, what would she do in that situation? And if we up the stakes a bit there, how would she then behave?" But almost never, almost never to illustrate a theory or to make a point. What I'm doing consciously and, I hope, unconsciously is telling a story, that's all. It's very gratifying and interesting and pleasing to find that you've done all these other things as well, but that wasn't what I thought I was doing.

MB: I suppose what I was thinking about was that almost unconsciously you'd found this metaphor of filth to describe the absolute opposite of what Dust represents for you.

PP: Yes, but it's quite an easy one, that, isn't it? I mean it's not hard to make an association between nasty, dirty things that smell bad and people who aren't very nice.

MB: But to link that with Dust, because Dust is . . .

PP: Well, I didn't!

MB: No, but I did!

(*audience laughter*)

MB: I want to talk about daemons now, which you brought up before. Shall I invite you again to tell the audience about the daemons?

PP: The daemons play a very important part in the imagery of the story, as well as in the—what am I going to call it?—the underlying myth of the story. When I began to write it I hadn't thought of them. I just had Lyra, the little girl, overhearing something she wasn't supposed to overhear and getting pitched into an adventure on the strength of that. It was difficult to get that going, though, because the first chapter simply consisted of her going into a room where she wasn't supposed to be and listening to something. That's rather hard to describe because you've just got the one character and you've got to tell the readers what she's thinking, so you say what she does and what she thinks and why, but it's rather awkward. It's much, much easier in a sort of simple, technical, storytelling way if there are two of them, because then they can talk, and one can say: "Let's go in here," and the other one can say: "No, we're not supposed to." And then the first one can say: "Well, don't be such a coward," and the second one can say: "Well, only for a minute." It's much more dynamic, there's a sort of dynamic relationship going on already. So as soon as I discovered that Lyra had a daemon I leapt on it for that reason, it made it easier to write that first chapter.

In the course of the first chapter I discovered more about daemons, because you don't make it up before you write it; you discover what's going on as you write it. I discovered that everybody in that world had a daemon, and the daemon had the form of an animal, and it had to stay close by. It was physically separable; my daemon might be sitting on the table there and could probably go as far as the wall, but no further, because it would hurt. And I also discovered that there were various social taboos: you mustn't ever touch somebody else's daemon—it's a gross breach of manners to do that. And they are all formed like animals. I could see at once this had all sorts of possibilities. It let me give an idea of a person's character very quickly. If someone's daemon is a snake, they're likely to be a different sort of person from someone whose daemon is a little bouncy dog, so you can say something very quickly about a character with this picture.

When I'd written that first chapter and established that everybody had a daemon, I also discovered in the first chapter that everybody's daemon could change shape from moment to moment, so one moment it could be a cat, and then a snake, and then a moth, and then something else. I don't know why I did that, but that seemed to be what they were doing, everybody's daemon, adults, children, everyone. Then I stopped, because long experience of storytelling has taught me a handful of things, one of which is that if you put something in a story that doesn't advance the story, it gets in the way. It's not neutral; it either helps clarify the story or it gets in the way. This idea of everybody's daemon changing shape all the time got in the way. I could look ahead and see that I'm not going to do anything with it because it doesn't say anything. If it's just a picturesque detail to get me started, then we'll soon get irritated with these daemons.

But then I realised that it was only children's daemons that changed shape; adults' daemons settle down in one fixed form and stick to that. *That* was the moment when I really realised I'd got something. I remember I was walking up and down the garden thinking this through, and I remember the very stone I was standing on when this idea struck. It was the best idea I'd ever had in my life! Instantly, I could see all sorts of possibilities that this opened up; and I was still discovering other things I could do with this daemon idea towards the end of the 1300 pages, or whatever it was, so it was a very rich idea. But people say: "Where does it come from?" I don't know where it comes from. My standard answer to "where do your ideas come from?" is: "I don't know where they come from, but I know they come *to*, they come to my desk." If I'm not there, they go away again, so you've got to sit and think.

MB: At one point in the novel you say that in one of the other universes, one of the universes where the daemons can't be seen . . .

PP: Ours.

MB: Our universe, the daemon would be "a silent voice in the mind", is that right?

PP: Yes.

MB: So it makes incarnate the idea that within our minds there are figures that are aspects or representations of ourselves. The daemons represent a more benign internal voice; for example, towards the end the daemons have to teach their humans how to be wise. I'm fascinated by the fact that in the novels there are also other internal figures which represent other aspects of the mind—not necessarily attached to particular individuals, as the daemons are very specific to each individual, but internal figures that I think all of us here would recognise.

The one that strikes me most vividly are the harpies. I find that whole episode in the third novel, the episode that I think of as the Harrowing of Hell, the descent into the underworld, absolutely the climax of the novel. If you link the ideas contained there with the daemons, it's very interesting. As far as I remember, the idea is that when Lyra goes to the suburbs of the dead, it is not only a terrestrial event but it's also a kind of metaphorical descent into hell, a "dark night of the soul" for them too. And the trial that they're going through is, amongst other things, about being separated. Can they bear the separation from their daemons? You've described vividly what anguish that is in physical terms, feeling wrenched apart—and it's in great contrast with the image of cutting which is also central in the novel. The cutting that's so horrifying is an absolute separation that makes the person dead; whereas the separation that you describe in the descent into the underworld is a separation in which the daemon is still very, very much alive in the mind of the children. That separation is not a cutting; it's a kind of separateness but "there-at-the-same-time". And by bearing that kind of separation, that kind of internal separation, without cutting, Lyra and Will grow in stature, grow in wisdom, so that by the end of the novel one of the witches says that they have become like witches—witches in the sense that the witch's daemon can travel a very long way from the witch, without that sense of internal separation.

PP: Yes. The world of the dead section was something I had been working up to. Now a lot of the things I'm saying this evening I'm talking about in terms of storytelling, because that's my central preoccupation. I think about this in terms of how I would write a story. If you put your character in danger in Book I and you have more danger coming in Book III, then it's got to be a bigger danger, otherwise it doesn't work in storytelling. And the only thing I could think of that was worse than the dangers they'd already faced was the danger of death itself, so that's the first thing—they've got to go to the world of the dead. Why? Well, Lyra in the first book has led a little friend of hers towards his own death, as she learns. She thought she was bringing him to safety but it turned out she was leading him into the worst danger he could face and he dies. She feels remorse about this and his ghost, if you like, visits her in dreams and says: "Lyra, Lyra, come and help me get out from this terrible place," and so she decides she's got to fulfil her promise to rescue Roger and go to the world of the dead and help bring him out if she can, or at least apologise, go there and say "sorry".

Stepping back a bit into the storytelling business, when I first thought of the witches I wanted to find some way of indicating that they had a quality of the uncanny about them, something strange and a little frightening for ordinary people. And given that I had this idea of the daemon that can't go very far from you, I thought: "Supposing a witch's daemon could, supposing you could see a witch's daemon without the witch. You'd feel a little shiver of fear: this is uncanny, this is too strange, I can't believe what I'm seeing." So I established the fact that witches' daemons could move a long way from where they were, and that's the part of the thing that makes witches different from us. I didn't know why, it was just there for that reason.

Now back to the entry into the world of the dead sequence. I discovered, I didn't know before Lyra and Will got into the little boat that was going to row them, I didn't know they would have to leave their daemons behind, I hadn't the faintest idea. But they get in the boat with the old boatman and he says: "He's got to stay, he can't come." And suddenly Lyra realises what she's doing, but she's made a promise and she can't break her promise to Roger. She's already said to Iorek Byrnison, the bear, that if you make a promise you've got to keep it. What a terrible dilemma! And so she has to leave her daemon behind, and Will and the other two companions, the little Gallivespians, the little spies who ride on dragonflies, they discover too, as the boat pulls away from the shore, that they've got daemons, but didn't realise this, because they feel this awful heart-wrenching, sickening, deadly, life-sapping pain as their daemons are pulled away from them. So that's what they learn, and they go to the world of the dead, and eventually are reunited with their daemons, who have not been killed but are still alive, but who have suffered dreadfully themselves. And then I realised what I could do with this, because at the very end of the story the witch is speaking to them and she tells them that this is how witches' daemons are able to separate from them: when witches are being initiated they have to go to a part of the Northland where no daemons can go. It's a horrible place, bleak and empty, and the witch has to go across it alone, leave her daemon on the nearside and this terrible, heart-wrenching separation gives the daemon the power to range freely but still remain attached. Thus Will and Lyra have gained something by doing this terrifying thing that caused them so much suffering. I didn't know that. There are a lot of things you don't discover but, if you leave enough loose ends lying around, one of them will fit, one of them you can tie up with something. So that's how it came about. Again not clever planning, just picking up the loose ends.

MB: I, like you, believe that the unconscious does its own work.

PP: Oh all right, fair enough! The unconscious hasn't yet asked for royalties, that's all!

MB: There's always a first time!

(*audience laughter*)

MB: I was also struck by the parallel theme between what's going on in the internal life of Lyra and her daemon, and what's actually going on for Will at the same time. You were talking about Will discovering he had a daemon when he feels the parallel pain and doesn't know what it is; but there's another pain that he's experiencing at the same time, and throughout the novel, and that's the separation from his mother, whom he keeps constantly in his mind while going through these terrifying experiences. It's interesting that in that kind of double separation, where Will is away from his actual mother and Lyra is away from, or at a huge distance from, her daemon, who seems to represent almost a wiser aspect of herself—it's then that they're confronted with the terrifying harpies.

PP: Yes.

MB: Who are figures in the mind, who are also internal figures. I think that all of us in our worst moments know what it means to have harpies in the mind.

PP: Yes.

MB: Perhaps I'll let you explain about the harpies.

PP: Yes, the harpies are of course the traditional figures from classical mythology who figure in this dreadful wasteland of death, and whose function it is to persecute you, make your life a misery, and torment you and frighten you and shower you with excrement. And so I was not doing anything especially original in putting harpies there. The twist I realised I could make with it again has to do with storytelling. All the way through, Lyra is presented as someone who tells lies, who tells fables and fantasies and spins yarns to keep people entertained, and when they first land on the shore of the world of the dead she thinks she can buy her way out of this difficulty by telling the harpies a story. So she begins by telling the harpies a story that she's just told very successfully somewhere else, a sort of fantasy about her life and her childhood. But instantly the harpies don't like it, they fly up to her and they shriek "liar, liar, liar", which echoes and sounds like her name, Lyra, so it doesn't work and she's bereft of the one power she thought she still had left, which was the power of telling stories. But they've escaped from the harpies this time and find their way into the world of the dead and meet the ghosts of all the millions of children who have died. These children have forgotten what it's like to be alive, they've forgotten their names, they're ashamed, some of them, to have forgotten their names. But the one thing they would love to remember is the physical sensation of being alive, and feeling the sun and the wind and the air, of being outside, and they beg Lyra to tell them about this: "Remind us, tell us what it was like, you've just come from there, tell us, tell us, we're longing to know."

So Lyra finds herself compelled by this request to leave fantasy behind and become a realist and tell true stories about what it really was like to be alive. She's got a store of experiences because she ran wild in the streets of Oxford where she grew up. She had fights with the other children, they ran about in gangs, they did all sorts of things. So she just tells them about what it was like to have a battle in the mud by the river. And what she describes are the physical sensations of feeling the mud under the fingers and smelling the smell of the river and hearing the rustle of the leaves, all the physical things, bringing the world alive again. When she's stopped, when she's told them this story, she looks up and sees to her astonishment that the branches of the dead tree under which she's sitting are thronged with the harpies who are listening. She says: "Why didn't you fly at me like you did before?" They say: "Because we didn't know we wanted this, we want this, we want to hear more of this, we want to hear true stories."

So they make a bargain with the help of the little Gallivespians, they make a bargain with the harpies that from then on the harpies have the right to demand of every new ghost that comes down to the land of the dead that he or she should tell the story of their life, the true story, true things. You have to notice the world and come down there with a story to tell; it doesn't have to be a dramatic story but it has to be true. It doesn't have to be well constructed but it has to be full of things that can feed this hunger for reality, for truth. And as a payment for this, if you tell your story to the harpies, they will then lead you through the land of the dead to the place where your ghost can come out and dissolve, not live forever playing a harp or something, but dissolve back into the air, be free of death and come back into the world of life to be, as it were, recycled. That's what happens in essence in the world of the dead, and I'm glad you feel that's a central part of the story. It is for me, it's the very heart of the story.

MB: I was thinking that the harpies themselves, like the Spectres, are another kind of emanation of this deadly force that can turn what is good into what is bad. For example you could look at the daemons as a kind of good conscience, or a good superego in analytic terms; on the other hand, the harpies do what *ought* to be good but actually isn't. After all, they are also in a sense looking for truth, but the kind of truth they're looking for is . . . merciless, cruel, they "shame you up".

PP: They "shame you up", that's the phrase one of the ghosts uses. They remind you of all the shameful things you've done, all the things you'd love to forget, they remind you of those, yes. I think you had a phrase back then which I mentally raised a little flag at, which was they're "an emanation of the force of darkness or evil", I forget how you put it, something like that. It's easy to fall into what seems to me to be a trap of thinking that because there are evil things, and evil things are done, and these things are done by those, that there must be an abstract force.

MB: I don't think so, no.

PP: But language lends itself very easily to the expression of that sort of way of saying things and I don't find I can believe that. There are evil people who do evil things; while there are people who do evil things and sometimes do good things. It's hard to call them evil people, you know, it's difficult. What I do *not* believe, explicitly and quite clearly and strongly do *not* believe is that there is a force of evil and a force of good of which people or imaginative creatures are merely the agents. I don't believe that.

MB: I'm not suggesting that either, I'm not talking metaphysics, I'm talking at the level of metaphor.

PP: Yes.

MB: As a metaphor, it's one I find extremely useful, no more than that. I wanted to pick you up on Lyra giving up the fantasy. The other thing that she seems to have to give up in the resolution in the novel is her magic. Maybe magic is not the right word. I can see your eyebrows rising. But if we take the alethiometer that she uses, I think you say she's able to use this wonderful instrument of truth by a kind of grace, and it seems that it's operating on two levels. One level is at the level of myth, this is necessary to guide the story. But there is also a non-mythical, ordinary child in Lyra. And before the loss of her childhood at the very end of the story, she has to give up this implement, which enables her magically to know things, and to start again as a little girl who has to learn from scratch. It's tremendously moving in the second of the novels when she tips into Will's Oxford and suddenly she doesn't know what jeans are, and she's walking into the road and can't cope with the traffic; and this little girl who's been a princess, an aristocrat, suddenly finds herself like a little lost girl who has to learn things from scratch. And there's a wonderful kind of metaphor in there too of a child growing up in a world where magically you believe that it's yourself that brings things about and very slowly you discover that life is very hard work.

PP: Yes, that's a very clear account of it. I'll go back to Kleist here and his essay *On The Marionette Theatre*, because his point is partly that. It's a wonderful piece of work, this essay. It's only 1000 words or so but it says more in that 1000 words than I said in over 1000 pages. What he's implying in that essay is that although we lose something at this stage of our lives, we lose this grace, this sort of innocence, belief in magic if you like, it isn't all a loss, it isn't all to be regretted and all to be deplored. The writers of the so called golden age of children's literature about the beginning of the 20th century, people like J.M. Barrie especially, A.A. Milne, Kenneth Grahame, seem to be caught up in this notion of this wonderful state of childhood after which everything is just dust and ashes and "nothing to be enjoyed at all since I was a little boy and playing with my teddy bear."

MB: It's like the Fall from the Paradise Garden.

PP: Exactly. I think that's not a state of mind that it's healthy to grow up in. It seems to me that we're better off embracing growing up and coming to terms with it and seeing what advantages that can bring. And so Lyra loses the power to read the alethiometer almost without thinking about it; but she learns, and we learn through her, that it's possible to regain the knowledge. The knowledge is not lost, the knowledge is still there, it's in libraries, it's in the experience of those others who know how to read it, it's in books and, though it will take a lifetime and it will be very hard work, concentrated intellectual toil. It will be full of passages that feel empty and sterile where she'll feel she's not getting anywhere, but it will be illuminated as well by certain accesses of understanding. And in the end she'll read the alethiometer just as well as she ever did, in fact better, because she will now understand why these connections work as well as just seeing that they do. This is my sort of optimism about growing up. It's not something to be regretted, it's not something to be deplored, it's not something to say: "Sorry God, I'm growing up"; it's going to be very hard but it's certainly going to be worth it. There's a metaphor, and we're talking in metaphors because this is a story, it's like losing grace but gaining wisdom—you can't gain wisdom until you lose, that's the way it works.

JC: We're about half way through and I'm sure you can imagine that it's very difficult to break into this conversation and at the same time want to keep it going, but I'm aware that there must be many of you in the audience who also would like to be more actively involved, so I'm hoping that we can manage to do that. There is a sense, as I think both speakers have touched on, that we're all actually discovering this world or these worlds as we go along, and that there is an open ended process for the author as well as for us, the readers; so in a sense it is an open book. I would like to open it up now to contributions from the audience.

Audience: I was wondering if you could say a little bit about the role of the Church in the books. It seems to be that they're just a huge source of repression. Perhaps you could talk about that a little bit.

PP: Because of the sort of moral reversal that we began by talking about in the understanding of the Adam and Eve, the loss of innocence story, it seemed a way of making it coherent, to follow that through and see that the Church is on the side of all the repression, all the death things. And it isn't really hard, if you look at the history of our own world, to see how you could understand it like that. The sort of stick I get from the *Catholic Herald* and places like that is because they claim I'm libelling the Church and that I don't say anything about what good the Church does, and the Church is all about love, and I don't mention this and I'm very wicked because I don't. "Up to a point" is my response. It's very easy for the Church to forget—or those who are devoted to the Church to ignore—the fact that the Church, all churches, not just one church, but all forms of organised religion, have really been perversions of the original teaching of their founder, and ways of establishing and maintaining a temporal, secular, political power for those who are in charge. They do this by repressing everybody who doesn't agree with them; they burn them, they burn them at the stake, they hang them, they throw them into prison, they forcibly convert them, etc. The history of the Christian Church alone is one of almost unmitigated horror. Those people who are closest to the teachings that you can read about in the New Testament are often the furthest away from the organised structures and power in the Church; it seemed to me that that was worth saying.

MB: Corruption.

PP: Well, Marie said "corruption" again, and of course the old saying "all power corrupts and absolute power corrupts absolutely" is very clear to see in the history of organised religion.

Audience: My sense was that the books all have aged with the children, that the books themselves become more adult in the way that they are written and more adult in the plot. Is that something you would agree with? And if so was it conscious? Were you aware of it happening?

PP: That's an interesting point. Certainly, the preoccupations of the central characters grow with them. It is, after all, a story about growing up; it's a story about leaving childhood behind and taking on the challenges and the difficulties of adult responsibilities; it's moving towards that. It's also true that the first readers were growing up too, because if they were 11 when the first book came out, they were getting on for 15 or 16 when the last one came out, so inevitably they were growing up. That wasn't a consideration that had much effect on the way I wrote it, it just happened like that. Is the book getting more adult? Yes, I suppose that's true. One reason that children have read it all the way through is because they can sense that they're in the position of Lyra, who doesn't fully understand everything that's going on; she herself is puzzled, tormented with fear and doubts at times, but vastly, powerfully, magnetically intrigued by this adult world that is somehow going on around her. And because the young reader trusts Lyra, and they can see that she doesn't fully understand, they're willing to follow her through and to discover what is going on. That I didn't realise either, until I saw how it had happened.

JC: Just before taking another point from the audience I wonder, Marie, you were saying at one point earlier that you thought there was an interesting difference between Will and Lyra in terms of their age and experience and understanding of the world, which seems very relevant to the point that's just been made, and I wondered if you want to say something about that.

MB: I was very struck that although Will and Lyra are apparently the same chronological age, Will feels to me to be very, very much older. I think it touches on what we were talking about a few minutes ago, to do with Lyra giving up her magic whereas Will in a sense has never been in that magic. When we first meet Will he is very grown up, he knows about responsibility; and more than anything he knows about loss, because he knows about love. He's had parents, and in a sense he's lost both of his parents; whereas Lyra has not had parents. She's had more or less good substitutes but she's actually not had someone who really put their arms around her until she meets Iorek the bear. They seem to me very different in that way. Lyra learns about love and learns about loss.

PP: Yes, that is true. Will's situation is this: his father has disappeared, vanished when he was a tiny baby, so he's been living alone with his mother. At some stage in his childhood, when he was about 7 or 8, he began to realise uneasily that his mother wasn't functioning very well, she was confused about things, she had imaginary enemies. But the one thing he could work out for himself was that if this became known, she'd probably be taken away and put in a hospital and he'd also probably be taken away. Will doesn't want that—the last thing he wants is to be separated from her. He thinks he can look after her, and we can see that he does, with enormous patience and skill and courage too, and dedication. One of the witches in the second book—witches have this power of becoming invisible, which isn't true invisibility, I call it a sort of "fiercely held modesty"; they can make themselves unobtrusive so that people just sort of look past them—the witch looks at Will and sees that he also has this power to an even greater degree than she has, and she's awe-struck by his power, because what he's done is to conceal himself and conceal his mother and just to act as if they don't really exist because they don't want to attract attention. From time to time his mother has a sort of crisis and he has to look after her, make sure she doesn't get out without being supervised, and so on, but nobody else knows about this; he's looking after her entirely alone. Now there *are* children like this, there are situations like this, and I'm awe-struck by the courage of these children. That was the origin of Will's situation and as a result of this, of course, he's had to grow up, he's had to become very alert to all the dangers and all the difficulties of the adult world and find ways of circumventing them and diverting them, and becoming invisible. So he's worldly-wise in a way that Lyra hasn't had to be, that's the difference. But he's still a young child really.

MB: He's more than worldly-wise, he's also terribly sad.

PP: Yes he is, he's never known what it is to live for a moment without responsibility on his shoulders, ever since he was seven or something. What brings about his appearance in the story is a sort of crisis. He suddenly needs to find out, for reasons of the story, he suddenly needs to find out where his father is, why his father is where he's gone, and so he sets off to look for his father and he has to leave his mother behind, that's almost like being separated from her, but that's what brings about the story.

I was conscious as I was doing this that I was writing against C.S. Lewis, who in one of the Narnia books has a little boy whose mother is dying. The little boy goes into the world of Narnia and there's a magic apple tree. He learns that if he takes one of these apples home to his mummy she will live; but good boys mustn't touch it, and if he steals the apple he will be a bad boy. So he doesn't. He goes back home and, because he's been a good boy, the magic of the apple works; and he gives it to his mother and his mother eats the apple and lives. I think this is about the falsest, filthiest lie you can tell. I mean it! It is a disgusting thing to say to any child that their mother's survival depends on whether they're a good boy or not, it is wicked, almost wicked beyond belief. How anybody like C.S. Lewis, who writes a story like that, can be hailed as a great Christian I do not understand. It makes me passionately angry. And so I wanted to write against that. There is no magic apple. When Will goes back to his own world, his mother is just as ill as she was, but what is different is that there is now human companionship. He's got a friend now, he's got a grown up friend, Mary Malone, who will be able to find a way of dealing with things that is a proper, grown up, realistic way that reconciles Will with the real world. So that's what I was doing there—kicking C.S. Lewis!

Audience: I just wanted to respond immediately to what you said about C.S. Lewis and that apparently awful story. Because if we take it from the point of view of the internal world of the child, we might think about it differently. We might think about this little boy actually faced with the wish to make his mother better, to cure her, and faced with intolerable conflicts internally about how to do that. It's not a story about what this boy should be doing but a story of his internal dilemma, which is dreadful. The outcome of the story is the fulfilment of his wish, that his mother has been cured by him choosing the right way. And of course what we do know is that children often feel very responsible for what their parents are up to, whether they're bad parents, whatever it is, and in their almost magical omnipotence they can feel they are to blame for everything. So I have a rather different reading of the story that you just described.

PP: Well, thank you for that, and I quite agree with you that children do have this sense of enormous responsibility, but to exploit that in order to make a religious point seems to me where the wickedness lies. There are no magic apples in real life. When people are ill they get better either because the resources of their body are rallying or because of medical science, that's why people get better, not because of miracles or magic apples.

To imply that there are magic apples which are available if you are a good boy and not if you're not seems to me, as I say, verging on the wicked.

Audience: Could you say something about the functionality of the parallel other worlds?

PP: Yes. The story takes place in many different worlds, well in about three or four, but the implication is there are uncounted billions of them. This is a very good device for a storyteller because if something is going awkward in this world, you just step through to another one and it's all right, you see! Magic apples, if you like. But of course you always take the burden of your difficulties with you and you can't escape them. You have to go back where you came from, and in fact at the end of my story all the windows have to be closed and we remain where we are. The Kingdom of Heaven is dead; if there is to be heaven it has to be a republic of equal citizens and we have to make it where we are, there ain't no elsewhere, fundamentally. But the "many worlds" theory, I believe, has a sound basis in physics and mathematics and so on, which I can't understand because I can't read the equations. However, I've read the stuff in between the equations and I think I can understand it in the works of people like David Deutsch, for example, who has written a very interesting book about it. It does seem to have some basis in physical theory. We can't ever really go to another world, but there seem to be other worlds which explain various anomalies in experiments on the quantum level.

But my interest in it was as a storyteller. Many, many stories begin by leaving this world and going into another one. Alice in the first book goes down the rabbit hole and she's in Wonderland; in the second book she goes through the looking glass and she's in the looking glass world, where everything is backwards and things don't make sense. In the book of C.S. Lewis, of course, you go through the back of a wardrobe into the world of Narnia. It's also in science fiction: you go in a rocket and go to another world and there the adventures take place. It's a very common storytelling device, and I was using that. The advantage of having many worlds is that you can have many kinds of pictures. One of the worlds I described is a world where the Fall never took place, where the creatures have attained a sort of wisdom and yet retained, as it were, their innocence. So I was using the different worlds to say different sorts of things.

JC: I'd like just briefly to add something to that myself that follows on from the question about parallel worlds, and links back to the point that Marie has been bringing out about the sense of coming to terms with loss, and with reality, at the end of the book; and your point that there are no magic apples there. At the end of the book, although this extraordinary range of worlds with their extraordinary properties has been explored, and even new relationships of love have taken place within worlds other than one's own, at the end, as the angel Xaphania explains to Will and Lyra, they have to go back. And they've seen it coming, they know they have to go back to their own worlds and remain apart. I remember when you came to Manchester shortly after the publication of *The Amber Spyglass*, and you spoke at a meeting where quite a number of people in the audience actually felt really angry and hurt that that was the end that you had given to the novel, and why did it have to be like that? It was only when I was reading the novel a second time recently that I understood, or thought I understood, the explanation you gave at the end of where the Spectres come from. If I understand it right, what you're saying is that each time a window is cut with the subtle knife between this world and another one, not only—and we can take a window as being, in metaphor, the operation of the imagination, that one is entering imaginatively into another world—not only is a window created through which one can step, but a little bit of the abyss seeps in through the join and breaks off and forms a Spectre.

To me this is a new idea. I said at the beginning that I thought psychoanalysis and psychoanalysts have something to learn from your work, and I feel this is something that I'm in the process of learning. There's an idea there which to me is new, which is that there is a downside to an act of creative imagination. To every act of creative imagination there is a downside which has to be taken account of; and the only way of taking account of it is by a return, a repeated return to the reality out of which one goes in order to imagine.

PP: Yes, because this is where we live, not somewhere else. We visit somewhere else in imagination but we can't live there; if you do live there you become something that's cut off from real sources of life, your energy becomes attenuated—it's not a real state of affairs. We've got to live here. This is where we live. And if we spend too much time in trying to travel back and forth there's a cost. The inventors of the subtle knife live in the world where the city of Cittàgazze is situated, where Will and Lyra meet at the beginning of the second book, a world where the inhabitants have to flee every so often because the Spectres come. They acquired or developed this extraordinary tool that can cut through between the atoms of the air and open the way to other worlds, but they used it for no better purpose than "stealing candy", as somebody puts it in the book. Instead of using it in a way that was informed by conscience, by a moral understanding of the importance of learning, they just used it to get, as it were, cheap energy, or to exploit things without putting anything back. That was the cost. And there is always a cost.

Audience: I just wanted to ask two questions, one about clean-liness, and the other one about the alethiometer. The alethiometer seems to me a sort of parent, like a lost parent that Lyra has lost, possibly like Will has lost his parent. And also another question about cleanliness. You [i.e. MB] were talking about things smelling bad, being dirty, being evil, but I don't think that's entirely true. When Lyra comes back from the station she talks about being dirty and smelling, but being quite positive about herself and going on and still feeling very warm, even though the other children are quite clean but aren't coping as well. And the first thing that Lyra does when she goes to Mrs Coulter's house is to have a bath with all these shampoos and expensive things try to wash away this smell. Maybe it's the smell that's real, it's a dust that's smelly but it's good. And all the characters like Lord Asriel and Mrs Coulter, they seem to be very clean and good people, whereas Lyra is very dirty and smelly but still very real.

PP: Thank you for that. That's very interesting indeed. Now one of the things that happens when Will comes across Lyra in the cave—she's been kept asleep by her mother who's trying to prevent her from growing—is that just as she's waking up Will relishes the warm smell of how she's waking up; there's an emphasis on the physical all the way through the book, this is where delight lies. Will delights in the smell of her, not because she's dirty but because she's alive, because it's flesh, as they delight later on in the sensation of their first kiss. The physical sensation, that's what they delight in. So that's a very interesting point. Thank you for raising that, because I hadn't considered it quite in that context before.

Your other comment about the alethiometer being a sort of substitute parent, that's very interesting. The alethiometer is a device that tells the truth, a sort of compass that points to truth. What Lyra does is to arrange the hands of it to point to any three of the thirty-six symbols around the edge, and there's another needle which is floating freely and which darts around and points to others, and that's how she understands it. I based this really on the medieval and renaissance notion of the emblem book. Now an emblem is a little pictorial device, a very common one. A very popular emblem was a helmet, a discarded helmet from a suit of armour surrounded by a cloud of bees, and this is a moral meaning, you see: out of the elements, out of the instruments of war can come peace; the bees have made their nest in the helmet and are making honey—*de bello pax* is the Latin inscription on that one. These were very popular, these emblem books, and it was an entirely different way of thinking from our modern way. There was one meaning which the emblem had and it's explained in the text: the goat means "lust"; the anchor means "hope"; and so on. That's how you are to understand the picture. I thought it was a very interesting way of getting at meanings, and so that's the way the alethiometer works. Each picture has a whole range of meanings, a dozen, maybe hundreds or even thousands, possibly, and by becoming familiar with that range of meanings in each symbol, that's how you understand it.

Lyra does it, as I was saying before, almost unconsciously by grace; later on she has to learn to do it consciously. It's a way of interrogating the universe; and we have various ways in our world. People claim that you can do this with the tarot cards or with astrology, or with the Chinese *I Ching*. These are ways of looking for patterns in the flux of things where you can't normally see patterns. You look into this system of patterns and it helps you make sense, but you don't have to believe it to use it. One of my favourite quotations is from the physicist Niels Bohr, the great quantum theory man. Somebody said to him: "Why do you have a horseshoe nailed up outside your door, you don't believe in that, do you?" and Bohr says: "Well, they tell me it works whether you believe in it or not!" And I don't believe in any of these things, but I'm quite happy to use them and see what happens.

MB: I wanted to ask you something on the alethiometer. Could you say something about Negative Capability? This is a concept my colleagues and I find very helpful.

PP: Lyra has to get into a particular state of mind to use the alethiometer; she has to be relaxed but attentive. Not wandering, but not screwed up either; it's a subtle thing, and it takes a while to get into it; once she's got into it, that's the state of mind in which she can see all these ranges of meaning. In *The Subtle Knife*, in the second book, she meets this scientist from our world, an ex-nun and university teacher called Dr Mary Malone, who is researching into dark matter. She's a physicist and she's discovered that she can contact some entity, some consciousness it seems to be, if she goes into this similar state of mind. Now because she's come from our world and she's old enough to have read the letters of John Keats, she recognises in something that Keats was saying, 200 years ago or so, exactly this state of mind. Keats was talking about the state of mind in which you have to be in order to write a poem—Negative Capability, "being in uncertainties, mysteries, doubts, without any irritable reaching after fact or reason". You have to be able to move about in the twilight confidently, without anxiety; you have to be able to watch things out of the corner of your eye without turning the lights on, because if you do, they vanish. Now I'm aware of this because I do it all the time when I'm writing a story. There are some ideas that come to you and they're just shimmering there, but you don't want to look too closely because they'll vanish; just let them come and get gradually closer and closer and they'll emerge. So it was a state of mind that was familiar to me, a wonderful description in the passage of Keats, very famous, so when Mary Malone quotes this to Lyra, Lyra knows at once that's what she was doing. She later tells Will, whose power is the Subtle Knife, that he is doing the same thing, but he didn't know that that is what he's doing. So that's what I say about Negative Capability.

JC: I'd just like to add something to that, because you may or may not know that the very same concept, and coming explicitly from the very same route, is actually much talked about by psychoanalysts and by psychotherapists, particularly in the last 20 years; and it's often taken as an apt description of the state of mind in which the analyst or the psychotherapist working psychoanalytically tries to be in order to do his or her work . . .

PP: Interesting, yes.

JC: . . . in being with and listening to and observing a patient in the consulting room, listening in an open-minded way, with what Freud called "evenly-suspended attention", which means being patient and waiting, and not "irritably reaching after fact or reason" about the patient's mind. And it's actually very frequently quoted in analytic literature, and it obviously has a great deal of life as an idea among our professional community. The concept appears in two or three places throughout the book explicitly: it appears with Lyra and the alethiometer; it appears, it seems to me, with Will and the use of the subtle knife—in order to be able to cut with it he has to be in that state; and it also appears explicitly with Mary Malone when she's working out how to put bits and pieces of stuff together to make this thing which is called the amber spyglass and will eventually enable her to see Dust. So I wonder also whether this capacity which you referred to as a "fierce modesty" . . .

PP: A fiercely held modesty . . .

JC: . . . a fiercely held modesty of the witches, or Will's capacity rather like that to be inconspicuous, whether these could be regarded as a kind of active form, if that's not too paradoxical, of Negative Capability; a way of being-in-doing which enables something to remain not too severely provoked but actually listened to.

PP: I hadn't made that connection. It's very interesting to hear it from you, thank you for that. Yes, it could well be; it's a state of mind which those who know it recognise at once, and those who don't know it think you can measure and test. I was trying to describe this once to someone in education, and trying to explain that this is what happens when you write a story. If you want children to write stories, somehow you've got to build this in or build in the opportunity for them to understand it, and instantly he thought: "How can we test this, how can we make sure that?" Well you can't, you cannot.

Can I just say something about Mary Malone, since she's been brought up. The other day I had a postcard from somebody who said "Dear Mr Pullman, I don't know whether . . ."—what did she say?—". . . a friend of mine told me I should read your book, I am an ex-nun teaching at university, and my name is Mary Malone."

(*audience laughter*)

PP: What's going on, you know?

MB: A parallel universe!

PP: That's what I had to say to her in the end. No, she was a Canadian teacher, not of physics actually but of theology, but she had left the Catholic Church about 6 or 7 years ago and caused a bit of a stir in Catholic circles in Canada, which I didn't know about. Anyway, she was amused by this and wondered if I was using her name consciously. Of course I wasn't, but that's coincidence. I mean, if you want to make up a name for somebody who's likely to have been a nun, it's not a bad choice, is it?

(audience laughter)

Audience: Authority hasn't been mentioned. It seems to me that one might say your opinion is that all authority, or perhaps authorities are bad.

PP: The Authority, capital A, is what I call, what the characters in the book call, the old idea of God, God the omnipotent Father, the Creator, etc; and he's represented as being a force of repression and a being in whose name cruelties are carried out and power is wielded. That sort of authority is clearly characterised as bad. There are other kinds of authority which I suppose you could read into the book if you looked for them, and you could find that the authority of someone like Iorek Byrnison is another sort of authority: he has the authority of physical power, but physical power tempered and moderated by responsibility. The authority of scholarship is embodied by the master of Jordan College and later on by Dame Hannah Relf, the principal of the college that's going to be Lyra's home, which is called Saint Sophia's, the college of wisdom. So there are various kinds of authority which are benign. It's not all authority which is bad, that would be foolish. Authority which is justified by moral qualities or by learning is, I think, given a measure of respect.

MB: And it's more a personal authority.

PP: Yes.

MB: And Will has the right to use the knife because it's his responsibility.

PP: That's right, yes.

Audience: Could I just ask, your mentioning the story about Mary Malone made me remember that I'm very interested in the choice of the names you've used for the characters. Could you say something about that?

PP: Yes, I've told Marie this story. I did a talk, well, it wasn't a talk, it was an interview, not unlike this sort of situation, at a conference in Oxford not long ago on the subject of child psychotherapy, and somebody asked me a similar question. Somebody had read a paper pointing out that the name of the witch Serafina Pekkala sounds not unlike the Latin *pecca*, sin, and I was making an association between witches and sinfulness and so on, and I said: "Well, actually no; I got the name Serafina Pekkala, because I wanted a sort of Finnish-sounding name, I got it from the Helsinki telephone directory."

(*audience laughter*)

PP: And the reply to that was: "Of course you thought you were, but your unconscious mind was prompting you to choose that!" So, you know, you win either way with that one. But yes, when you're telling a story some of the names come without any effort. Lyra was always Lyra from the beginning, I don't know why. Lee Scoresby, I found his name—he's the balloonist who comes from Texas—the Lee part of his name comes from the actor Lee Van Cleef whom you'll remember if you know that Clint Eastwood film *For a Few Dollars More*, the best of the spaghetti westerns. Lee Van Cleef plays a sort of tall, lean bounty hunter called Colonel Douglas Mortimer, who's got this wonderful range of guns, and he has a terrific duel in the street, he and Clint Eastwood; so that's where the Lee comes from. Scoresby comes from the Arctic explorer William Scoresby, and there's a Scoresby

Point or a Scoresby Bay in Greenland named after him in our world, so Texas and Greenland together make Lee Scoresby. Some of the names you make up, some of them you just find and some of them your unconscious tells you to pick out of a telephone directory.

Audience: You said earlier that you didn't originally plan to have daemons in your book, and they just came to you and you incorporated them into the story. I was wondering why you chose the word "daemon", because although it's spelt differently, it's pronounced the same as the conventional meaning, which is often evil or a bad spirit, but in your book it's the good side to your personality. It was something you said about comparisons with the story of Genesis—I thought another comparison would be with the snake as sort of [*inaudible*]

PP: That's a very good point, that hadn't occurred to me at all, that's very interesting. Why daemon? Because that's what I found my pen writing, but actually the word has got a history, it comes from the Greek word *daimon*. Socrates, for example, talks about his *daimon*; it's something like a cross between a conscience and a guardian angel. It's not clear really, but that's where the word came from originally, and it seemed to be a good word to use in that context. The only people who are troubled by that are people who haven't got the patience to read the little introduction at the beginning, I think. I could have called it Lyra and her goblin, or something, or made up a word, but then making up a word is always a bit unsatisfactory. There are only a few made up words in the story and they're there because there wasn't a word for them; or else there was a word but I wanted to use it to indicate a difference—like the word "anbaric": there's a moment when Lyra refers to an "anbaric" light and Will says: "We call it electric," and she says: "Electric? No, electra, that's that golden coloured stuff that you rub," and he says:

"That's amber," and they both say: "Amber, that's where it comes from," and they both understand at the same moment. This is what I meant earlier on by saying that children follow things they can't understand because the people in the book can't understand it either, and then they work it out and they see it as well.

Audience: One of my favourite characters in the book is Iorek the bear, and I've been feeling slightly disappointed that we haven't talked more about him, but one of the things that occurred to me as you were speaking was that perhaps you were Iorek the bear.

PP: Well I'd never thought of myself in that role. Iorek is a protagonist in the story; I'm the storyteller. My wife sometimes compares me to a bear, but I think on the grounds of short temper rather than any other qualities. That's a new one on me, you've thrown me with that one! The role I feel for myself, just to finish what I was saying about being in the story, is the person who's fascinated by the business of arranging all these incidents and these events and putting them in the best way to bring out the connections between them, and then telling them as clearly as I can. That's what I like doing, that's the only role I have. I like to keep myself out of the story as much as possible.

JC: I think that's the point where we're going to have to stop. It seems so arbitrary. It seems so arbitrary and so cutting, I have to say, to cut this, which could go on for a long time. I never thought I would compare an audience in a meeting I was chairing to all the dead sitting round in hell, but actually that's the vision which I had growing, the rapt attention of these faces. And of course, in the scene in hell all the dead gather and are just spellbound, and the harpies too, you suddenly realise, are sitting somewhere!

MB: And the persecuting audience has become benign.

JC: And the persecuting audience has become utterly benign. So it remains really only for me to extend the warmest, warmest thanks to Philip Pullman for coming here. Philip has to go and talk in lots of places and I imagine he could get very tired of it, and we are very, very grateful to him for coming and being so open with us; and to Marie Bridge for starting the conversation before today with Philip, and for carrying it forward and for opening it up for us. And you're all very welcome now, if there's space, to join us for a glass of wine, which is going to be down there in the sunken area, or fruit juice, probably, or water, failing that, and take a look at the book stall. There are a few copies for those of you who haven't yet got your copies of *His Dark Materials*, and thank you very, very much.